Grasshopper

The poetry of

M A Griffiths

arrowhead
poetry

First published 2011 by
Arrowhead Press
70 Clifton Road, Darlington
Co. Durham, DL1 5DX
Tel: (01325) 260741

Typeset in 11 on 14pt Laurentian by
Arrowhead Press

Email: editor@arrowheadpress.co.uk
Website: http://www.arrowheadpress.co.uk

ISBN 978-1-904852-28-5

Printed by MPG Biddles Ltd., King's Lynn, Norfolk.

on behalf of the author

this book is dedicated to the memory of her
deceased mother

Marjorie Mary Griffiths (née Westall)

Preface

Next week will see the first anniversary of Margaret Griffiths' funeral. I posted the following tribute on my website a couple of weeks later. It is pleasing to note that after less than a year many of the hopes and wishes expressed in the piece are about to be realised. Concerns about copyright have been overcome. Thanks to Arrowhead Press a substantial collection of Margaret's work will appear in book form and following the efforts of a small, but dedicated group of 'mazfriends' from across the English speaking world, much of the poet's work has been rescued from oblivion. I was pleased to be able to contribute to this project in its early stages by tracking down links to the eighty or so poems ensconced in the Sonnet Board's archives. My efforts were richly rewarded; I was given access to the developing on-line archive. After just a few weeks of concentrated 'cyber-archaeology' on both sides of the Atlantic over 300 poems had been re-discovered.

Margaret tended to post material in differing styles on a variety of internet poetry sites. So, although she had many admirers, no-one, I suspect, truly appreciated the range, variety and volume of her output until the bulk of her extant work had been collected together. As I read through scores of poems that I had never seen before I became increasingly convinced that, taken as a whole, her work was substantial and significant and the efforts to collect and preserve the material were simply the first step towards ensuring that Margaret's talent became more widely appreciated. When Roger Collett, editor of Arrowhead Press, asked me if the personal recollection that I had written just after Margaret's death could be adapted to form the introduction to a forthcoming collection, I agreed immediately. A few words would seem to be in order to explain how the original piece came to be written.

As news of Margaret's death spread across the internet, fellow writers were moved to post memorial poems at Eratosphere and elsewhere. I simply could not find the right words. Instead, the day after I received the password to Margaret's on-line archive I decided to write a personal tribute – 300 words or so – that I could post on my website. Hours later, in the small hours of the following morning, I found that I had written something ten times longer than I had first intended. The result was part tribute, part obituary and part critique; admittedly, it was hardly impartial, lacked academic rigour and gave insufficient weight to Margaret's achievements in free verse. However, perhaps it did capture the great sense of loss felt across the on-line poetry community at the time and reflected the growing realisation amongst her many admirers that Margaret was not just a pioneer amongst internet poets, but also a writer of broader significance whose contribution to contemporary British poetry had yet to be fully understood. I am certain that publication of this collection will help to rectify the situation and Margaret Griffiths' work will begin to receive the wider recognition that it undoubtedly deserves. *Alan Wickes, Buxton, 30th August 2010.*

Goodbye Grasshopper – a personal recollection.

In July 2009, BBC radio's current affairs programme 'File on Four' featured 'funerals without any mourners' exploring the increase in funerals for people who have died alone with no known next of kin or family. What is tragic, the programme revealed, is the sometimes painfully long periods before such deaths are noticed. When, on 12th August, the body of Margaret Griffiths was discovered by police at her home in Poole having lain undiscovered for some time, it would be so easy to slot the event into the narrative of this bleak social trend. No relatives could be traced. Margaret's funeral was sparsely attended, only a few neighbours and the solicitor entrusted with winding-up Margaret's modest estate gathered at the graveside on September 7th. Undoubtedly the extraordinary reaction on the internet a week or two later when news of Margaret's death was reported on the poetry web board 'Eratosphere' would have astonished this small band of mourners.

Although her talent may have been little appreciated locally, Margaret Griffiths had a reputation as a poet which spanned the English-speaking world. In 2005 she was named by 'The Academy of American Poets' as one of the greatest internet poets. This was not an accolade which Margaret would have sought, for although she was a keen participant on internet poetry boards, edited the poetry ezine 'Worm' and had occasional pieces published in print magazines, she kept her personal life to herself and sought anonymity rather than fame. Moreover, she seemed almost wantonly unaware of the extent her abilities or of her growing reputation amongst fellow writers.

An unfortunate side effect of the poet's belligerent modesty was a tendency to mislay great swathes of her own work through a variety of computer mishaps. In the weeks since her death a concerted effort has been made by admirers and fellow poets to collect her work, published in print or on-line, to create an indexed archive of the poet's extant work. With the assistance of magazine editors and the moderators of the web's leading formalist poetry boards such as Gazebo, The Sonnet Board and Eratosphere, the aim is to publish Margaret's work in book form and bring to the wider public and literary establishment a better understanding of Margaret Griffiths' much overlooked talent.

After only a few weeks over 300 poems have been tracked down, some finished, some in the making, gleaned from workshop archives. Early publication, however, is fraught with difficulties. It is less than clear to whom this considerable body of work belongs as no living relatives have been traced and, as you might expect from the poet's unassuming character, she gave no regard whatsoever to the fate of her work after her death. I suspect she would have treated the notion of needing a literary executor with a characteristic hoot of derision.

Given the tragic manner of her passing it would all too easy to characterise Margaret as reclusive and anti-social. However, to those of us who corresponded with her on-line, 'Maz' as she preferred to be called, was clever and funny; her approach was kind-hearted yet quick to unmask pretension. In workshops she proved a canny critic; as editor of 'Worm', an email based poetry ezine that ran to 40 editions, Margaret treated all contributors with equal respect. Many aspiring poets, myself included, are indebted to her ezine as a place that was willing to print poems by complete unknowns.

Those of us who communed with Maz in the odd and somewhat hermetic world of cyber-poetry will mourn the passing of a pioneer, a delightful spirit and a generous critic. It is Maz's poetry, however, that will be her lasting legacy. It is only as the larger body of her work is gathered together that the significance of her writing becomes ever more apparent. Margaret's talent was wide ranging, her work eclectic; if she had been a chef, then fusion would have been her forte. Her on-line 'handle' was

'Grasshopper' an apt avatar for a writer who never stayed still, was equally at home with free verse or formal, whose poetry ranged from the screamingly funny to the darkly disturbing. Her manipulation of language enabled her to write at times in styles that bordered on the archaic, yet never descended into pastiche; she was inventive enough to produce nonsense poems that revelled in the street language of imaginary sub-cultures or dystopian distant planets.

Above all else Margaret Griffiths' poems are a joy to read, morsels to savour, little gems of poems that glitter with invention – vivacious and immediate. In 'Cutlet, Mince of Denmark' she cooks up a synopsis of Hamlet in 14 lines. Appropriate to a revenge tragedy the action seems to have been re-invented in a butchers shop. The concluding couplet gives a flavour of the whole concoction, exuding a relish for language and a sense of humour not averse to the occasional excruciating pun:

The thyme is out of joint, and drumsticks thrum.
Did Bacon write this tripe? The butchers come.

I first became aware of Margaret's work when I started to post my poems on 'The Sonnet Board' some years ago. Maz was a moderator. Her advice and thoughtful criticism proved invaluable; above all else the range and variety of the poems she posted provided exciting and challenging models for those of us trying to hone our own sonnet writing skills. Perhaps her most celebrated work in this form is the superb 'Opening a Jar of Dead Sea Mud'. The simple act of removing the lid from a facial product provokes a recollection of painful childhood memories. The sonnet concludes with a striking image of the jar as a metaphor of suppressed anxiety:

I close the jar, but nose and throat retain
an after-tang, the salt of swallowed pain.

Unsurprisingly, Richard Wilbur picked out the sonnet for particular praise in Eratosphere's 2008 annual 'Sonnet Bakeoff'. The 'Spherians' themselves voted the poem overall winner. Margaret Griffiths was well recognised on both sides of the Atlantic as a gifted and versatile writer.

Like D. H. Lawrence, Maz wrote wonderfully about animals and birds. Domestic pets appear in her poetry as important members of the household. In ' Ding Dong Bell' she assumes the persona of her cat to take a wry sideways swipe at the absurdity of her overanxious preparations for a dinner party. Initially the cat observes, with wearied derision, his owner's frantic preparations:

the bedrooms were a whirl of cloths and mops,
much bathroom bleach sploshed all around the bends,
great waspiness of Hoover on the stairs.

Later, you sense the cat's growing disapproval, a burgeoning feline jealousy at unfolding events:

She's donned a dress, a closet lecher's dream,
the pristine kitchen's pregnant with fine food,
the startled rooms and furniture all gleam.

Finally the cat, usurped by unwanted human intervention in his domestic domain, wreaks revenge:

Ding Dong. Her guests arrive in festive mood.
Ah, that's my cue to squat with blissful hiss
and souse the Persian rug with pungent piss.

The piece is typical of Margaret's lighter verse; it unmasks human foibles with empathy and understanding. Her humour is based on wry observation; it is never cruel or destructive. As in all of her work she reveals a natural talent for the well-honed phrase – 'great waspiness of Hoover on the stairs' – in the context, it's simply 'spot-on'.
In case the few facts we know about Maz's life – that she seems to have lived alone with a collection of domestic animals, that her death went un-noticed locally, that she seems to have had few face-to-face social contacts – tempt anyone to invent some kind of buttoned-up spinsterish existence for her, then the energy and humour of 'Ding Dong Bell' must lead you to quite the opposite conclusion. Maz came over in all my dealings with her

as funny and outgoing, yet honest about her fears and anxieties. She had one more quality in common with D. H. Lawrence – Maz wrote about sex... quite often, sometimes with disarming candour.
In 'Advice from Mother Goose', the ghostwriter of Perrault's fairy tales opts to give impomptu advice to her younger female readers.

> *Holding frogs and newts*
> *takes skill, as slippery as an eel's ringed squirm:*
> *a female art, my dears, that bears rich fruits.*
> *The needful squeeze is confident and firm*
>
> *to seize control, but not so tight it hurts –*
> *so wise princesses earn their just deserts.*

If we try to seek out common threads in Margaret's varied work then the preceding poem touches upon what seems to me to be a recurrent theme. Many of her poems explore the female psyche through figures derived from myth, folklore, fairytale and legend, often using dramatic monologue. Often powerful female archetypal figures take control. In 'Hippolyta at Dawn' the Queen of the Amazons dominates her lover:

> *He sighs, he yields; this skirmish ends so soon.*
> *Engagements call me from the field for now*
> *so battle royal should wait till afternoon.*

'First Woman' celebrates Lilith as Adam's mate before Eve, a mysterious, powerful presence:

> *As Lilith prowls her realm, the night yields stars*
> *to settle in her hair like sleepy bees,*
> *and by their light, she counts the latest scars*
> *gouged in the planet's pelt by human greed.*

In other poems male, demon-like creatures hound the female protagonists, sometimes, as in 'Demon Lover' to comic effect:

I knew you were a demon when your eyes
went black and something vipered into view.
Of course I felt a soupçon of surprise
but Honey, what the hell, I still loved you.

However, in 'A conversation with the dark' the fears are more palpable and a sense of terror threatens to overwhelm the poet's characteristic poise:

You sit like dust again behind the door.
I yank it wide to seize your hair, and roar,
I have you now! And slighter than I knew.
It was your shadow I had feared, not you.

Given Margaret's interest in 'mythic women' it is interesting to speculate on the question of her relationship to feminism. In poems such as 'The Women's Circle' she mocks the popularist, stereotypical image of the feminist. However, given the way Hippolyta rubs shoulders with Lilith and the Daughters of Ariadne in Margaret's work, it is almost inevitable that this aspect of her work will be placed within the broader re-examination of the representation of women in myth which occurred in the latter part of the last century.

Margaret Griffiths avoided speaking in public about either her life or work. A rare exception occurred when she agreed to be interviewed as the Poetry Kit Featured Poet in July 2001. We learn a few tantalising facts about the person behind the poems, that she was born in central London, that she'd visited relatives in South Wales frequently as a girl and came to love nature and the countryside. Interestingly she reflected:

'I suppose the biggest single literary influence on my childhood was one of my father's friends, a writer of elegant social history, who bought me books every time he visited. They were wonderful illustrated books about the Greek Myths, Tales from Shakespeare, the Arabian Nights, Perrault's Fairy Tales. Later he brought me classic novels, reference books and dictionaries. I would often pick a dictionary as bedtime reading, as I found words so fascinating.'

Perhaps the most telling statement in the interview is, in fact, the opening sentence:

'I hope that with all my poems, whatever else I am trying to communicate, I will communicate some of my delight in language and the magic of words.'

To me this sums up the essence of Margaret's gift. Whereas many of us work over a long time to find a particular poetic voice, Margaret was much more interested in experimenting with radically different voices and personae in her work. Her facility in this respect was remarkable.
In 'Family Feeling' she creates a kind of faux street talk which seems to languish half way between 'The Sopranos' and Raymond Chandler:

So Bobby has the case. The trouble is
it's not his case. Who did the switcheroo
and when? On Bob – my tricky dick, a Wiz
who fixed scores coast to golden coast – and who
could match his balls, who beelined all the biz?
So I can't trust him now? My number 2.
Sweet Jeez, we had it stitched, the fuse had fizz
but now the nose-cone's in the shit. What's new?

'Spaced' recreates within a few opening lines the 'space-punk' world of Hans Solo's Millennium Falcon or Bladerunner:

Carpenter rode the starstorms round the outer rim
of Ryga, traded blue-rockers and wreckers
and the real estate of dreams. He hard-hustled

with the skin tribes who ply, Altair to Actureus,
and mojammed all the dives that stud the systems,
sawing mean riffs on the Les Steele cithern.

Yet Margaret also revelled in rich, romantic diction. The following lines from 'Longing' would not seem out of place in a late Victorian piece. They have a fin de siècle yearning about them, a century too late:

At last I wearied of desire, and grew too tired
to hope. The business of the world, its grind
and grief, devoured my time. Grey sirens mired
my course and I was lost, but now I find
your presence at my side, where you have always been,
to crown me with the stars that I had never seen.

She wrote extensively about scenes from history and revealed in later years an enthusiasm for a lost medieval world of chivalry, hunting and falconry, such as here, in 'The Duke A-Hunting':

She cuts the morning wind, a grey-fletched arrow
dispatched to strike the prey. She stoops, kills cleanly,
then mantles jealous wings to claim the sparrow.

Her ability to write convincingly, apparently at will, in a bewildering variety of voices made Margaret wickedly good at parody. When 'The Sonnet Board' became even more besieged than usual by egomaniacal poets with a penchant for posting risible 'traditional sonnets' in the style of Shakespeare or Keats, Margaret parodied their efforts in 'Casting Pearls':

These Creatures value not my antique jew'ls:
"'Tis not contemporary speech." they cry.
I write for the Elite, not vulgar Fools;
The more I Shakespeare ape, the more Bard, I.
Enough! I have great Sonnets to compose.
Bring me my quill, my doublet and my hose.

Given Margaret Griffiths' versatility, it is no surprise that when her death was announced on Eratosphere contributors recalled with fondness a wide range of poems that had been workshopped there over the years. One title, however, kept recurring, – 'The Bateleur'. There is much in the poem that typifies Margaret Griffiths' art. The subject matter seems both ancient and modern simultaneously. The sonnet itself is wonderfully organised, metre, form and meaning honed into a rich amalgam. Most of all the poem is beautifully phrased:

She landed there
as softly as a stork re-sits its nest.
She gazed at me and I absorbed her stare.
She preened her wind-combed quills, then came to rest
sphinx-still, her eyes a blaze of feral gold.

Maybe it seems far-fetched to suggest the way the startled eagle settles upon the poet's ungloved wrist is a metaphor for the power of art over nature, nevertheless there is something mythic about the bird's return. It is a magical piece in the best sense of that over-used word.

I still can't quite believe that Maz has gone; I am still shocked at the circumstances of her death. What happens now? I have no doubt that the copyright issues will be solved in time. I am confident that a small press will be pleased to publish a selection of her poems, they will be well received and her reputation will continue to grow. What I fear is that the grim circumstances of her death may overshadow her life, that she will be cast as a latter-day Emily Dickinson, a fine poet little known in her lifetime but much appreciated after her death. But Maz was nothing like that. Her situation is more analogous to the Arctic Monkeys circa 2003 than Emily Dickinson in 1886. In other words Margaret Griffiths is not an undiscovered poet, but she may be the first major poet whose reputation on her death was almost entirely based upon her web presence and not on print versions of her work.

What would I like to happen? In five years I would like to be browsing in the poetry section of a Waterstones store somewhere seriously unliterary like Ellesmere Port. Just before I reach the Faber collected works of Ted Hughes I would like to come across the Faber Collected works of M A Griffiths. Hopefully the plain coloured cover will be green – bright grasshopper green.

The poet should have the last word. Margaret did leave her last orders in sonnet form. Given the circumstances of her death there is a sickening irony about the piece, a tragic reminder that life rarely follows art. As for the poem itself, well, it's very 'Maz':

Last Orders – The Movie

I'm ordering a Hollywood decline.
The symptoms are ideal: not being sick,
the application of a pale lip slick,
some floaty scarves, a duty to recline
against silk pillows being brave, while friends
and family troop in with gifts and flowers
and wet-eyed memories of golden hours –
stock shots of surf and seabirds when it ends.

Spare me the vulgar things, like diarrhoea,
depression, pain; they're for the hoi polloi.
A dying will seems such a good idea:
I want a starry close, so please employ
soft-focus, and cue choirs' Ave Maria,
then fade me out with Ludwig's Ode to Joy.

Alan Wickes, Buxton

September 20th 2009

Acknowledgements

For Research:

This book was aided by fans who helped locate the poet's material on a bewildering number of extant and extinct online poetry forums, including: *Sonnet Central, The Poetry Kit, The Pennine Poetry Works, Burgundy, Capriole, P.O.E.M.S. Place, The Poetry Free-for-All* (at *Everypoet.com*), the *Gazebo* (of *The Alsop Review*), and *Eratosphere* (of the magazine *Able Muse*).

Special thanks to:

> Rose Kelleher
> Julie Stoner
> David Anthony

David Adkins – for biographical detail.

Frank Lane Picture Agency Ltd. – for the cover photograph.

Contents

12

copper wire (coiled)
briefcase (unlabelled)
shackles (well-oiled)

strap (for disabled)
tape measure (long)
twine (or strong thread)

leg-strap (strong)
white cap (for head)
two-foot rule (closed)

wrist-strap (pliable)
pliers (long-nosed)
rope (reliable)

12 Days

On the twelfth day of Christmas
my true love sent to me:

12 cells a-sleeping.
11 missiles cruising
10 gats a-rattling
9 dum-dums dumming
8 shells a-bursting
7 uzis pumping
6 mines for laying
    5 b o l t springs
4 falling bombs
3 French stens
2 pistol slugs
and a cartridge in a spare tin.

I said,
"Aw, Osama,
all I got for you
is a
small
box
of
hankies."

3 Mormons or Whatever

I was standing on a wide plain
scoured by dusty winds, when 3 Mormons
came to bury me. They had broad shovels
over their dark shoulders, and on each shaft
they'd hung a water-skin and a lantern.
The water was salt – their lanterns were unlit.
I lay down unresisting in the hole
they dug for me with murmurous prayer.
Under the sandy weight they heaped upon me
I slept a little. Slept and stirred and slept,
until the sound of their retreating boots
awakened me to a night of snakes and stars
and a small tan fox with a smiling snout,
with a tail as bold as Renoir's brush.

Ada and Evan

Before stereotypes had time to harden
Ada and Evan shared the Garden.
Ada said "I hope God understands
that Fruit just came off in our hands."

Arguing maturely "Did!", "Didn't!", "Did!",
They heard God's step and quickly hid.
"Now you are mortals" breathed God's voice
"and capable of moral choice."

Ada said "Knowing evil must be good;
We had to claim our humanhood.".
"I think you're quite right" echoed Evan
"We have to die to get to heaven."

"Yes" said God "You've done the Knowledge.
The Tree was like a moral college.
Well done on the the initiative test.
Now go forth, folks, and do your best!"

In the distance God espied
greed and gore and genocide.
God shrugged and murmured "Screw it.",
twitched Her robe and left them to it.

Advertising Arsenic

The image that sticks with me is Emma stuffing
whiteness into her mouth like sherbet powder.
She does it on the run, I think, her long skirts curling
around her legs like neglected cats. She swipes
her mouth with the back of her hand. Then she says,
half to herself, half to me: I will lie down now
and go to sleep. That's how we both want it:
the soft blink into a deep gentle end – but I know,
and how does she not know? – that there is pain
and retching, long hours stretched with suffering
till the body exhausts the light.
                                            Listen, Emma,
Woody Allen says he's not afraid of dying,
just doesn't want to be around when it happens.
We understand that, don't we? I understand you,
feel your desperation, the last leap into darkness
that turns out to be a flame. I would take your hand,
help you step over the stile of flesh into the green
and freedom of the next field, where they are picnicking
in a blur of meadow flowers. Instead we stick
here like flies nailed to a windscreen by a rush
of wind that chills our eyes.
                                            I will leave, Emma,
be gone finally, and you will always run and try
to escape. Your stomach will heave, your guts
will grind again and again, but you never lived.
You have that mercy, yet I cannot forget you,
cannot dislodge the teasel of you from my hair.
I carry your weight like an unwanted child.

Advice for a Wood Maiden

Walk softly on leaf-mould and do not crush
blue flowers. Be courteous to mice and squirrels,
tend the wounded vixen, de-thorn the she wolf.
Be merciful to spiders and ants, your small wise sisters.
When it is time, greet the dark crone
gracefully and accept her poisoned apple.

Polish it but do not taste. Cradle it in your right palm
till you see the red truth of it, blazon
on a robin's breast, the heart's echo, a swelling womb.
Hold it until it liquifies, a cleansing gout
that breaks between your fingers, drips
to the forest floor like tiny footfalls.

Bathe in the tingling stream and robe yourself
in white linen, woven paper-thin, and velvet
the colour of nocturnal grass. Scent your breasts
with sandalwood and vanilla seeds.
Touch your lips with the memory of blood,
let the owl's wing brush your temple.

Now take your reflection from the stream,
spreadeagle it with silver nails against the stars.
Once you have crossed the sky, mountains will kneel
in your shadow, the sun will kiss your toe-tips.
But all this matters to you less than the skill
of reaching into men's eyes and stealing thoughts

like tumbled stones. And all that matters to you less
than the moon's pull in your belly
and the beat of your sure bare feet.

Advice from Mother Goose

Today we'll talk of princes, pets, it's story time
and magic lurks in millponds. Here's a frog
cold-humped by well-wet walls: how such things slime
and slither, silver-muscled, damp as fog

and just as hard to grasp! The waking kiss
is easy – overstressed, I think. The lesson
is rather how to catch, how not to miss
a golden chance, and never mind the mess on

your dainty digits. Holding frogs and newts
takes skill, as slippery as an eel's ringed squirm:
a female art, my dears, that bears rich fruits.
The needful squeeze is confident and firm

to seize control, but not so tight it hurts –
so wise princesses earn their just deserts.

After

He thought about it for years
but there was always
some reason for delay:
after Christmas, after his birthday,
after he'd dumped his current.
Then it was after the wedding,
after the christening,
after nursery school,
always after.

After the doctor
had given him the news,
he thought of things
growing over years.
After he'd made the connection,
he picked up the phone
but then it was too late.

He added a bunch of flowers
to the supermarket trolley
and on the way home,
he parked by the cemetery
and left the chrysanthemums,
ferns and gypsophila
on a stranger's grave.

Aftermath

Enough. I have no stomach to defame
his memory. The man died well. Go, prise
the blazons from the walls and doors. My name
will over-write his wealth, my lordly rise
will soon erase his legacy and line.
Bring in my hounds, my hawks, install my pages.
Unlock his stores, uncask his finest wine,
unchain his chests to pay my army's wages.

My sword is stained with blood, indeed. No, leave
it so. They say good brands must drink their fill
before they sleep. That steel was forged to cleave
the armour of my foes, to carve and kill.

His family? Safe passage to the North,
except that one fair daughter. Bring her forth.

Afters

Unpeel me slowly, like the fruit
you placed on a white plate
ready to accompany the wine
or the cake, frilly-papered,
that you eyed while you ate
your salad and brown bread.

The apricot warms, ripening,
the cake crumbles in its case,
sugar crystallising and re-melting.
Taste me slowly. Let me melt
into the granules of your tongue
like icecream on shingle.

Make me zing like lemonade
after strawberries, like sherbet
on a rod of liquorice. Make me
flesh and sponge, sweet
and sour, savoured, swallowed,
assimilated. Make me muscle.

Aftershock

No man is an island,
no woman is a rock.
We'll stand side by side together
and ride the aftershock.

To those who died in silence,
to those who died in screams,
we will dedicate our future
and consecrate our dreams.

For those who died in rubble,
for those who died by fire,
we will call peace to his kingdom
and build our towers higher.

For those who died through terror,
for those who died by hate,
we will guard our children better
for we share a common fate.

No man is an island,
no woman is a rock.
We'll stand side by side together
and ride the aftershock.

after Troy, after Tripoli

My sisters howled like Cerberus with all three throats.
It was from lack of loaves, the absence of love.
My brother was small enough to hide in the chimney,
but they smoked him down like a side of ham.
And I said nothing. I cricketed in the yard
for my mother, who was spread on the stairs,
blood drawn by the moon or the dawn's razor.

I teach my siblings cockroach instincts
to survive bird-torn days, blasts of black
and light, the sun in metal hands.
Our cooking pots bubble, meat bobs
in yellow juices. We eat anything, horse,
dog, rat, cats' tongues, offal, we sleep
in jackal packs and we will be waiting
when they return with their bottled grins
and gifts, with their red labels, their white
and ink, the green rustle in their pockets.

We are legion in the dust, fierceness turned
upon itself in woodlice balls, shells rolled
by the wind. A kick breaks us into jaws
to devour them, their money, their promises
and fat excuses. We will build seven hills
to crucify their beliefs. We will nail them
to the past. We will shit out their politics.
My father is unburied bones and their wives
will weep for strangers.

The Alchemist's Omelette

If he traces three more arcs, he will make a cat –
not a common striped creature like Arnolfini's
ginger tom – but an incandescent beast

with onyx eyes. Nim pauses, his horn-nib suspended
over the page, then inscribes two arcs
at the proper declension. The third curve tries

to draw itself. He hears the thin hiss as it sucks
at the Chinese ink, and then it crouches,
frustrated and invisible, a long quiver

in the air waiting for a weight of colour.
Around Nim, flickers prowl and growl
in unfinished flourishes, designs and devices

all requiring just one more touch suddenly
to be, to leap from some tangled dimension
into the simple now. If he closes his eyes

he can see scattered points of light.
They burrow beneath his lids and prickle
against the skin of his sight. He knows

eyes peel like onions, burst like ripe grapes.
Space, busy with nearly-but-not-quite,
presses around him with an undercurrent

of insect vibration. The sound grows louder,
breaks, concentrates into a small beat, tac
tac, the eggtooth of an unhatched chick

trying to crack its shell. The egg, that symbol
of perfection, which hangs above Piero's Madonna.
He curls his fingers around the smooth, cool concept

and smells incense. Once you are, he whispers,
you will die. Time has stronger magic than mine.
Without the last stroke, you have Forever.

The unpersuaded air tensions between chair and chair,
chair and table, like cittern strings. His mouth becomes
the hole in a sound-box, rounded by surprise

as four claws rip through incompletion like knives
through a curtain. A woman, with long chestnut hair
and skin as blue as gentian bells, is the first.
She leads a great lynx on a golden cord.

An American in Kilburn

The smoke threatens as you enter.
There are old words
in the corner, secrets dissolved
in glass, in the amber spirits
dark as a sick man's piss.
The ghost of sawdust lies shivering
on the floor, an old abandoned dog,
eyes bright and unforgetting.
Nothing is forgiven.

Seek your Oirish, fresh
from the Hollywood hills,
rub your plastic blarney
on his green back and Danny
will sing for anyone who asks,
his voice oiled by whisky,
rasped by smoke, the rebel songs,
sweet and sharp as a knife
through the heart, as nails
through the knees.

There is darkness here, of love
and country, the edged shadows
of cleared homes, the thin cries
of orphaned children, wordless
as sheep. All they wished to bury
in the peat has shouldered upwards,
following the generations,
staining new bones.

You of a young country,
you do not understand
the rivers that run deep
beneath the skin, the sins
punting teethed like pike
in the underground steams.
Lay down a mat of blades
and green divided leaves
and I will dance as Daniel sings.
I will dance right gladly,
sprightly as a fiddler's fuck.

The Angel of Mons

The Angel of Mons
who was not
furnaced in a sky
who did not walk
on mud sweating darkly
not with blood or bile
through clumps of hair
sere grass nor
bleached feathers
from his shadow
who did not weep
over the fallen
black tears like
poppyseeds
the Angel was not
imaged forth
in retrospect
was still and stillborn
as rumours of peace
spat square
into the ranks
of chill and cankered clay

The Angel of the Bottle

I found the plastic bottle
which you filled last week
in your jumbled bag.
When I opened it,
the water stank of something.
Only six days and the water's rotten.
> The Angel said Yes but
> it looks fine. That's the danger
> with water. I tried to tell you.
> The world is a place of
> deceptions floating on
> stale water. You need fresh air.
I poured away the stagnant liquid
The cleansing cold tap streamed and
bubbled till the stench disappeared.
> The Angel inclined his head
> humming, the scent of
> violets in his span.
You put the plastic bottle
into your jumbled bag.
Next week I will find it.

Annie

Annie went to work
for the nobs
up at the big house
said goodbye to her ma
and her brother
and sisters
packed a package
with very little
neatly and set off

She lived high
in the eyrie attic
shared a narrow bed
with a kitchen maid
up at six and work
till ten at night
one afternoon off
every two weeks
and think yourself
lucky, girl

She worked as a lady's maid
laid out the bright
and glittering dresses
for the daughters
of the house
most of all she envied
their lingerie
so smooth and sleek and soft
Annie's underwear was wool
and itchy

One day clearing
a bedroom grate
to build a fire
Annie found something
crumpled up small
a paper ball
She smoothed it out
on her morning white apron
and looked at
the one pound note
She had never held
a pound note before

It was three weeks' wages
she sat back on her heels
and held it
and she looked
and she wondered
she knew that sometimes
the nobs left money
around deliberately
to test the honesty
of servants

Annie took the risk
and kept her place
she didn't save the money
didn't buy something
sensible
on her next afternoon off
she went into town
to a Lady's scented store

In her drab dress
a sparrow
amidst the pheasants
she bought two nighties
straight from Paris
milky silky soft
when Annie wore them
she felt like the queen
of France

Annie and Dromida

He never used a cup
but drunk from a flared bowl,
fingers curved around the far side,
his thumb touching the top
of the liquid, then he tipped
the bowl and drank. After a while
she found handles strange.
He did not like hot liquids
or spicy foods that bit
the tissues. She found
that she gave up vindaloo
and turned to the sweet
and aromatic dishes, with lots
of plain boiled rice, pure white.
He confirmed what she had
always suspected, that
the last letters of the alphabet
were in the wrong order.
He had a red faded picture
of a stone light-years away that
proved it. His eyes were as yellow
as a wolf's gaze. She had sucked
barley sugar, sherbet lemons,
soft rich caramels. Her tongue
recognised the colour. His pelt
was flecked like a leopard's
and he preferred the shade.
She had never enjoyed sweating
in public. Their fingers
interlocked.

Apples

Five apples, red and green,
Swelling with summer sweetness,
Because the crown was plucked.

Because the crown was plucked,
Five apples, green and red,
Swelling with summer sweetness.

Swelling with summer sweetness,
Because the crown was plucked,
Five apples, red and green.

Aquarium

Remembering what never happened,
she cannot forgive him for the blue space between them,
for unshared memories, bright as the tank
of ocean fish he insisted on buying.
He godscaped rocks and plants into a waiting world,
then drove home flushed as a child at Christmas,
bearing the jewelled denizens like secrets,
and spilled them out into the ready-warmed water
in a sparkling climax. She remembers his face,
blurred by lust, his fingers curled and secure,

the smell of his heat. She lifts a brown cotton shirt
and brings it to her nose because it is too heavy –
the only way she can bear the weight is to draw its scent
into the centre of her. This is it. These are it – his things,
to be sorted, graded, sifted from her life. The yellow dog
bumbles in from the terrace, seeking something, then buries
his disappointment in a deep bowl of food.
She can smell the thickness of the gravy as his tongue
forages. She speaks a name softly and the dog
looks up, looks sideways, as if he heard sounds
outside. She hears nothing, but her eyes follow

his blunt hopeful movement, and something moves
like wings in her chest. She shuts the French doors,
bolts and bars them, checks the closure with fingertips,
as if struck blind. She would shut herself tight
if she could locate the fastenings, if everything
were not open, unfurnitured, if all the fittings
were not broken beyond repair. Behind glass

peaceful Chromi burn sapphire as they squarm
from weed to weed, angelfish sway together
like three a.m. dancers, paired cinnamon clownfish
bob in a sea-anemone. The dog rolls slowly,
takes possession of the Namda rug, and sighs.
His hot mouth perfumes the air with meat. A sleepy finch
calls from the chestnut tree reminding her of things
she would rather forget: dawn, the long day,
a new dark suit, the list of tomorrows in her diary.

Archaeology

Chink-chink, clunk-clunk, there's no escape.
You spade us from the ground, then scrape
our skulls and excavate our teeth,
spread naked what once lay beneath
mute earth. You want to learn our name.
Ah, we are levelled, made the same.
This bone-yard bursting at the seams
is one deep bed of blended dreams.

Our bodies are transformed and rotten,
and what you are, we have forgotten.
We wish to feed the shrubs and trees,
to nestle wild birds as they please.
We are all light now. Do not weep.
Heap heaviness upon us. Let us sleep.

Archery

I think you should have stayed alive,
breathed fast & slow, distressed your skin.
Instead you stand on youth like a dais

draped in spring – an arc of long bow
on your back & arrows in the quiver
of your lips. I circle you like an exhibit

but always look away before you speak:
the dead should have more decorum.
Mount the waiting grey, ride off into distance,

leave me to the present & my hours.
I do not wish to see your clear eyes
& your unlined flesh. I do not want

to remember time's promises. I cast
my bones as runes to rattle you away.
Remain dead, remain gone, remember forever,

& do not touch the bowstring. I have eaten
your arrows one by one. Their tips porcupine
my guts. Their shafts are leaks in my heart.

Ariadne's Daughters

Nasty girls make mouth music. They fist the air
and leap and shout 'Fuck'. They drink until they puke.
They spin and scrap and scrape denim till it bleeds.
They paint their eyes with clouds, and hoist hems
like brigantines tagging the trade winds.

All this with faces small and compact as auriculas,
sweet as the little monkey-smiles of pansies,
with tender skin, tight secrets, thousand island
juices. Sour and fruit as wine, old and fresh as Pinots
hanging in unplumbed air, near-bursting, trembling.
The moon strokes them, marks them with must.

When we remember, we fear for them and plait cages,
but they were born with feathered arms and sly fingers,
locksmiths, thieves, shysters, survivors. They crop
like shark's teeth and roll up the shore, down the streets,
dancing and laughing, bright with sun and soil.

Atlantis

We have lingered in the chambers
of the sea and heard from far above
reverberation of great storms,
thud and thunder
muffled by the mother brine.
I couch with my close kindred
in the rainbow coils of nautilus;
curved in the marble maws of conch,
we grow tentacles of will.

We are moulding limbs and weapons
with your old abandoned metal,
with heavy poisons jettisoned,
and the wanton waste of earth.
Thoughtless lands have taught us
to unshape and re-assemble,
We repair the ancient temples,
resurrecting shattered towers:
we have re-turreted Atlantis.

Scrape us with your greedy trawl-nets,
sound us with your subtle sensors,
we will keep our secrets still.
Here in the liquid caverns
where life first burst-bubbled,
slowly, deeply, we are transforming time.
While you hasten to conclusion,
we are moving to beginning;
while you scramble to your finish,
we are building into birth.

Bang

Last night they dropped
a nuclear bomb on Canford Heath.
Lying so near a port,
it always risks a strike,
and through the dry weather,
bored children burn small holocausts
between the gorse and bramble,
turn living wood to charcoal,
like angry minor gods.

I was at an afternoon party,
standing by French windows
framing sky. Something stopped.
My ears popped, and I couldn't hear
what people were saying.
There was just enough time
to gaze at each other
and gesture at our ears,
oh-ing like shubunkin, then

we knew and all dropped
to the carpet. In that instant
before the sun devoured me
I thought of the garden outside
the larkspurs, ladybugs and robin,
all innocent as Eden.

In reality, of course,
there would be no time
for theology

Bard Cheese

Last night in dreams I left my love abed
And stepped outside into a rose-rapt bower,
Where Philomel piped softly overhead
As fragrance breathed from ev'ry moonlit flower
and, sated there by Cupid's darkling feast,
I pondered sweets enjoyed and true words vowed.
I knew that Joy itself my joys increased,
and thought such golden gifts would make Gods proud;
And then beneath an oak, there grew a light,
Not of this mundane orb, but of the skies.
Great Phoebus stood, his glory dimm'd by Night,
And to my lover's casement turned his eyes.
I learned the mighty Sun waits on your lawn,
Since till you wake, the new day cannot dawn.

Bast

She has this sense sometimes
of men striding through the fields,
strewing words like dragon-teeth
to raise armies of spears,

while she is set to glean and gather,
to turn bronze points into grains,
and fill the bag of her garments.
She will keep her garner close, safe

from some imminent drought.
In her armpits, she suckles kittens
to rear as guardians for her granaries.
She feels the future like a swell

across the world, an undercurrent
slow yet gaining speed and anger,
rolling larger below the horizon.

She holds that soundless moment
before the blast, balled on her tongue,
caged in her teeth.

The Bateleur

She was returning to the gauntlet when
some dolt yee-hawed a horn. She slewed left, fetched
off course, alarmed, towards the misty fen.
I heard the sharp cries of the crowd, and stretched
my ungloved wrist out wide. She landed there
as softly as a stork re-sits its nest.
She gazed at me and I absorbed her stare.
She preened her wind-combed quills, then came to rest
sphinx-still, her eyes a blaze of feral gold.
The handler bustled up to break the charm.
He mentioned luck, unlocked her talon-hold,
and claimed the eagle from my unscathed arm.
Between her wingbeats, Nature spurned the rule
that beauty shows no mercy to a fool.

Beast

I'll take the beast out for a walk, beware
the prowling nose, the fangs, the eyes of fire,
the barrel chest and shoulder strength. Take care.
Do not approach too close and tempt its ire.
Velociraptor camouflaged in black
and henna fur, hair-primed to pounce and feed.
What holds this salivating terror back?
One hopeful human clutching one frail lead.

At home, a fast dissolve to precious ducks;
it's kiss me quick and tummy-tickle-rub,
all licky luvvy chops and finger-sucks,
wide liquid eyes that plead for woofie grub.

Part dragon wrapped in fur, part greedy hog,
part loon, part teddy; all beloved dog.

Bed Room

When his father left
she slept with the child;
warmth in place of heat,
tears instead of salt,
but they both woke her
with nightmares.

That bed a realm
of lost roads and cities.
In the cupboards,
strange monsters
and familiar smells.
We always hope
that children do not know.

Soon she will lie alone
and the boy will dream
under football banners,
circled by dinosaurs.
She will draw words
between her sheets
and shape a horse
to rock herself
asleep.

Beelines

Out of the drowsy singing vessel
comes the bee in neat-nap velvet
black and gold, armed as fiercely
as a paladin. She possesses what
I lack, the call of purpose. She mounts
the air, homing in on golden gales
of nectar trails, draws her sisters

to her treasure, dancer in the templed hive,
the singing dome, packed with shining wax
and generation's curl and clusters.
Out of the droning honeyed vessel
comes the bee, and another and another
on a quest through scented strata,
armed like knights, like amazons.

Out of the sleepy humming vessel
comes the bee, bright with purpose,
fast as a star in her instinct, signifying
what I lack. Sharp sister in the wind,
mistress of the sun, small dynamo
of summer. The power that I lack.
Out of the throbbing solar vessel
the sisters come, gold and black.

Before

She thinks of it as a small cauliflower, pale and pink-threaded like a peeled shrimp. In her dreams, the haulm divides into two brain-lobes which think of her as something smaller than a pea.

She wakes with a start and no appetite, and pulls on her underwear, which she checks compulsively, yanking the gusset wide and taut to search for scarlet. Then she twitches her bra straps, feeling her nipples cold and hard, afraid to feel them damp.

Emptying her bladder, she is aware of her centre, a medusa's purse, of pressure like a kidney stone, or the scrape of grit on an oyster's palate. She wants it gone, longs for the familiar void, the un-invasion of her womb, but she tries to stop thinking in case it hears her thoughts.

This period will not last long. Afterwards she will soak every day in passionflower and sage, until the jar is empty. Then she'll drop it into the rubbish bin and scarcely hear the muffled crash.

Bellerophon Before Breakfast

I am heaving my reluctant flesh around with me
as if I carry Quasimodo and his hump. I always
doubted that he could be so agile across the gargoyles,
though I saw him in black and white, his swinging progress
a mix of broken baboon and mounting ibex. As for me,
the spring in my heel has dried up. My elan has died.

I turn on my laptop and it responds with a small cascade
of notes, warm somehow, an emblem of pleasures to come,
like the flying horse that leaps across the cinema
screen while I'm settling back into the plush, holding
my popcorn like a talisman – or like that grey giantess
with spikes in her hair. But no opening credits blaze at me,
merely a mundane gape of mailbox, so I read the first,
or last, email. There must be a difference between them.

Now I am concerned. They want my help to find a child.
She has been missing in Ohio, in Denver and Detroit;
they have been seeking her in the canyons' cleft, across
the level gilt of prairies and Okefenokee's steam.
I see the sheriff who's in charge, know he's hitching up
vast pants to signal he's giving this search his all,
his rifle propped against brush-scratched chrome. I picture
a dandelion's head, its blonde tufts surrendering to the wind.

She was already lost years ago when I first logged on.
Should someone tell them that she will have changed,
grown fatter or more fleshless, or at the least,
older? It seems bad manners when they're asking for my help.
I am so far away, anyway, beyond the bleak Atlantic. Still
the distant problems reach out to me, and I can offer no aid.

The worry is that it worries me less than it did, as if time
has stretched one cornea over both my eyes, and clouded it
with a cataract, vicarious grief that has torrented
across the screen for so long. I have seen such things
that sight has turned in on me, a gorgon gaze
that petrifies soft tissue. Now I feel incredulity
at each new atrocity, but no longer any surprise.

I accept that an angel's apprehension ends, face-down,
arse-up, in stinking mud. Perhaps the stallion is more suited
to the air than a man. Pegasus will stride out of the myths
into the strata of the sky, and Quasimodo will swing
down ever lower, his tongue swelling, his words fading,
till the city's common breath turns his heart to stone.

Dark water reflects the clouds: I hear a small flip and flop –
frogs in the sucking sediment at the edge of a great lake.
The sheriff hefts his weapon, and the vehicle drives off
importantly. Overhead huge wings may thunder
but cameras are focussed on the exhaust-trail
wisping up the road and over the dark green horizon.

Beloved

He held the Beloved carefully,
feeling her weight, her promise.
She coiled around his waist
like his dead sister's arms.

Tomorrow, we will do God's work.
he murmured . We will go
to the marketplace, into the press
of people, so I can bring you

close to them, and you can bring
them close to God. With every step,
I will pray, and see the ache
in every face which we have come

to end. O Beloved, do not fail me.
In the last ecstasy of blast
and metal fused to flesh,
carry me to heaven.

Bereavement: a Survey from Apollyon

A) Did you hear old laughter in the sky?
B) What did you do that night e.g.
resort to alcohol? C) Did you try
to bury thoughts like old salts in the sea?
D) Did you whimper, whine, or did you howl,
a riven beast, then howl and howl again?
E) Did you stare at air? F) Did you prowl
the numb grey streets, your ribs scooped out by pain?
G) Did you doubt that any ache was worse
and any darkness deeper dark than this?
H) Did you rave at life, at God, and curse?
I) Did you fold and fail, you piece of piss?
J) What bore you onwards till this day?
Think hard, you worm, you coward – can you say?

Between the Lines

Darling, I do not know you but unsolicited,
you sent your heart to me in an email, popped it
out as readily as a tit from a small bra-cup
and opened your history to me. You are a pretty girl,
Russian, very nice.
                                    I'm sure you have exotic eyes
and English that halts as irresistibly as a limping Bambi.
Oh, I am ripe to be captivated, to be swept off my shoes
when you visit my city soon. We will meet
in my favourite coffee-house, intoxicated
by fragrances of Kenya and Java.
                                    I will give you
a precious phial of rose attar, pressed gently
from ten thousand crimson petals. Nothing
remains but for this curse of heterosexuality
to be lifted from my lap, like a fat stubborn cat,
and everything will fall into place.
                                    Soft kisses
from your friend, your passionate passport,
your beloved opening to the new worldly world.

The Biographer

How hard it is to write of death, when Death
stands at your rounded shoulder, bending near
as if to read the words. True, in the breadth
of mortal shocks, a death is nothing rare

yet you have lingered on his early life,
his word-plays, wit, and fame: the fairy-tale.
And how he sparkled, like refracted light
mosaic-ed on a Monarch's wing – and just as frail.

One lapse would brush him down to earth, and pin
him flat. Now follow that descent, record
the toll extracted by his fatal whim,
his end, no longer feted or adored.

You pen the final words: your subject's done;
Death dries your page with sand, and whispers, Come.

birdroom

somewhere in this room
there is a dead bird
four plump Java finches
perching yesterday
on the curtainrail
today an odd number
somewhere in a corner or
behind a piece of furniture
there is a dead bird.

I should look for it
but not yet
the green canary
bubbles with song
sends out a tendril
of notes so beautiful
it touches pain
one of the doves coos
with tender lust
a parakeet flirts
its vivid wings

I know somewhere
there is a dead bird
but I will not seek it yet
in the room of my mind
there are dark corners
where thoughts lie
desiccating like dead birds
I will not disturb them yet
not while sunlight
smells like honey
and canaries worship Pan.

Black Britain

Seventy percent of the clothes here
are black, he says.

Do not wear black,
he says, your eyes breathe it in.
It poisons joy.

Black gives you the blues and blues
endue black feelings.
He wraps himself in gold and orange.

On Mondays,
Moondays,
he wears grey and silver,

but never black.

Black Ribbons

Today they put black ribbons on the trains.
The dead are dead, the stricken try to heal,
the rest remains uncertain.
I have seen this before in monochrome
and technicolor. My mind is full
of eyes, intent, without a face.
Each time we think 'Enough',
but the engine moves along the track,
signals sound, steel sheers and buckles.

It comes closer, closer, till it arrives
within each one of us, a dark thing
on metal thighs with eyes we see
but do not want to recognise.
For all those who cry 'Enough',
today they put black ribbons on the trains.

The Blue Geranium

Enchanted by the picture on the label,
I bought the pack. Ah, those blue-eyed blue
flowers, profligate as grass seeds.
When I looked more closely, I could see
pale roots in the dry compost
fragile as dead babies' fingers
pressing against the plastic bag.
You have been neglected, my geranium,
you were prepared then overlooked.

I slip you gently into a white bowl
to soak in warm water. You are valued,
now, loved. Grow, you bugger, grow.
Star my summer with deep blue
and I will feed you, water you, protect
you from slugs and snails, I can do that.

Booby Trap

That roar should be diminished by long years
and not return as loud as the express
exploding through the station now. It clears
the platform, thunders through. Its scream grows less
and less, it draws away like one past day
with no known terminus. He won't confess
that still he hears and feels the blast, the way
his clothes clung to his flesh, his battledress

meat-soaked, smeared camouflage, the blooded cloth
spew-warm and wet. Shreds dried on him, no time
to waste, to wash, he had to shift, move off
across the tangled land, with that brown slime
across his chest, to save his men, forget
his friend, and later, hose him off. No sweat.

Breaking the Habit

Helen always loved her son.
She tried to like him when he turned
to drugs and snarls and slouches,
when he stole from her purse
and her house and her friends,
when he turned to wider crime
to fuel his habit, because his father
had left when John was twelve
and that is such a traumatic age
for a boy.

      For years she loved
and opened to him whenever
he came knocking. Sometimes
she paid his debts or his dealers
or his bail. Sometimes she nursed him
when he paled and puked and shivered.
Once she brought white powder for him,
her lungs tight and hot.

Now she never sees him. Last year
he wrote her a letter pressed black
with hate. She tells everyone that
he was a changeling and the elves
took him back to fairyland.
When people say, "Really?",
she replies that it is not a fact
but in every other respect, it is
completely true. Then she smiles
like a slice of lemon.

Burden

I am so happy with my words,
I keep them in a cage like birds.
I feed them dandelions and seed
and find there's little that they need.
I change their sand-sheets every day.

In case they want to fly away
I leave the cage door swinging wide
but they sit peacefully inside
the bars, and bathe and preen and sing.
I love my words like anything!

Butterfly Bawl

This Pinkerton's a bearded porcine prig
and Butterfly's swathed in a dressing gown
with corsets and a weird tarbaby wig –
make-up à la Marceau or Glock the clown.
They all strut stiffly in that Operatique way
with sudden dashes to stage left or right,
but with the first sweet strains of 'One Fine Day',
cool cynicism yields to glued delight.

My eyes leak gently, from hope's anchorage,
till Butterfly lies with her heart torn out,
amongst strewn petals on the darkened stage.
The curtain falls. I'm harbouring a doubt:
How would Pink's folks regard that little chap,
half Yankee Doodle Dandy, and half Jap?

Calling the Roll

As another full year ends,
let us salute our absent friends

Count Tosselkov who modelled pollen grains to scale in wax,
Whistle Murphy, who married seven women, each five years
younger than the one before, Cardinal Dab Brockney
who catalogued the thirty-nine sexes of angels,
the Michel-Burkiss twins who circumnavigated the globe
each year while they lived, and were scattered
on the trade winds when they died, Ram Shah Pann
who enamelled his virile member with turquoise and pearl,
Ishmael Serif who perfected pellucid dreaming, Colonel P.D. Beeds
who could see colour with his finger-tips, Pierre Chamberlait
who conversed with molluscs, the Whittaker cousins who sighted
the first green mammal before they were lost in Sumatra,
Sugarcane Smith who wrote a twenty-three volume Epic
of the Great Venusian Wars and burnt it immediately,
Red Haslam who bred flying saddlebacks, James Wade
who invented stained-glass bullets, Rabbi Hyram Hite
who proclaimed that Doubt is the true foundation
of Knowledge, Trapp von Cutler who abducted aliens,
and Sydney 'Slim' Milch who pioneered the No-Food Diet.

Please charge your glasses, gentlemen;
we shall not see their like again.

Carnival

Through unmarked years of tables, chairs and chests,
did Christ the artisan live hormone-less
and haunt his body like a distant guest?
Or was he raised at dawn by lust, to guess,
when harlots brushed by in their drunkenness,
what painted lips and ready throats expressed?
Did he feel once the prick of sinfulness,
and touching hot temptation, whisper Yes?

And did the Devil set no fiercer test
when Jesus wandered in the wilderness?
What truths did wolf and jackal tongues confess,
and did he raise his splintered hands to bless
torn ewes, the eagle with her bloodied breast?
Who taught him that long howl of tendered flesh?

Carrier

My dog is a carrier, not of disease,
but of bits and pieces, scraps, snippets, litter,
torn cardboard, notepaper.
Some are rescued from the fliptop bin,
dampened lovingly, sucked for lingering traces,
some found adrift, air-lifted, fostered.
Ah, how the transparent case holds the essence
of chocolate ghosts, the intimate juices
of discarded tissues, the syrup of a sugar-bag.
I, with my rubbish mentality, wonder at
this bliss of littleness, tastiness of trifles,
significance of nothings.

I clear away. She exhumes, redistributes,
attentive, soft-mouthed,
a muscular re-cycling unit, warm, inexorable.
If God exists, may he/she lift me from the heap
of throw-away, and mumble me into a word.

Casting Pearls

As Shakespeare wrote, forsooth, so shall I write.
His hem up lifting, I'll his robe assume,
My verse infuse with his poetic might,
And mind me not that Moderns fret and fume.
Like Circe's pets, they scorn my polish'd feats
And grunt at each inversion and elision;
Such Swine will call Time-temper'd touches cheats,
And claim Tradition's sweets may need revision.
These Creatures value not my antique jew'ls:
"'Tis not contemporary speech." they cry.
I write for the Elite, not vulgar Fools;
The more I Shakespeare ape, the more Bard, I.
Enough! I have great Sonnets to compose.
Bring me my quill, my doublet and my hose.

Catching

3 am finds him at the fridge again,
interrogating the milk. He knows there is a moment
when its sweet turns to stale, sugar breath to meaty.
There will be a glow within the opaque plastic container, candle-bulby,
and a faint buzzing, easily missed within the condenser's
constant hum. At this instant the change will come as a spirit
released – this is how fairies have been seen, he explains,
the intimidations of decay – the blur of transformation mistaken
for wings. Each organic thing shedding its small nature, discreet
and discrete. Once he saw a lactic sprite at its business,
and large moth eyes fixed on him accusingly before it fled
across his shoulder. The next time he will be ready
to pin it smartly to the wall.

I persuade him to a pill, open the laptop
on his long game of Civilisation, pull, push, provide
a warm drink, and sandwiches of fresh white bread.
I display the excised crusts for examination. He opens
the rounds, inspects the cheese with eyes and nose
for signs of death, then eats.

I feel a presence in the air, a miasma.
Malaria was blamed on bad air – mala aria –
from the swamp, not on winged hosts. Contagion
that insinuates into the lungs, like the back-up
of a fucked flue. I won't smell it. It will get me, molecule
by molecule, snuggling into my alveoli. They will find me,
stiff, cherry-red, blushing at this embarrassment of madness
– not mine, not mine, but it will finish me

just as he captures a whirr of change between
his palms.

Chester Arnessy explains religion

Jimmy Bole had a bad eye from the war. The iris
rolled up into his skull, and left the bulge blank.
It looked sinister, but you knew it wasn't meant.

When he served nails and bolts and tools,
it was hard not to gaze into that white space.
I wrenched my sight back and concentrated

on the glittering green eye, that saw. It took
determination, real focus. Jimmy died of a heart attack
last fall. His store was taken over by a chain.

Now young men with two good eyes flash
slick smiles and don't know much. I saw
Jimmy's niece going into chapel. She stopped

and chatted. I looked at the big oak doors
but didn't follow her. God has only one good eye,
and I've always been talking to the other one.

Christopher Robin Muses on Religion

Sometimes I don't like you, God,
and think you are a wicked sod,
with laws about revenge and ire,
and heaping coals to stoke the fire.
They say you are enthroned above
in cloudy realms of peace and love
and yet of course you fully know
about the shit that's slung below.
You're not as blameless as they claim.
I think you have another name.
I think you are both dark and light
and creep about in secret night
with Satan's horns and twitching tail,
and chuckle when your creatures fail.
I think you are a wicked sod.
Sometimes I don't like you, God.

Christus Sissifactus

I knew his toes were pedicured, his feet
long, like his limbs, though
Josephus says that he was squat.
I saw him in my Bible, the nose
aquiline, never hooked, the Gentile-est
of Jews, a pale Pre-Raphaelite saviour
in freshly minted nightgown,
soft Dickensian eyes brimming
with masochistic Messianic rapture.
Hoist his hems and he'd be
smoothly forked as a Kewpie doll.

Too many images of a desert dandy,
Christ the simperer, Christ
coiffeured with pageboy bob,
designer-sandalled, perhaps
a stroke of kohl, a dab
of myrrh, Emmanuel who wouldn't
shrink from a little moisturiser
to counteract the sandy winds.
No wonder Nietzsche despised
the dim defeated wretch.

But what about Spencer's Jesus,
thickset and Semitic? By God, that Christ
might have roared, have done dark deeds
when the sun slept, turned the Red Sea
into burgundy and drunk and belched
and farted like a dreaming dog. That Christ
who cradled scorpions in his palm,
could suffer like a man and bleed
real blood instead of watered wine.

That man, with rough love, could hoist
the world upon his shoulders
and grunt like Atlas. A man like that
could make the Mount his sermon, resurrect
the temples and hammer stars back into place.

Chrysalis

Do not stand by a grey graveside
and mourn for one who's gone.
Death splits the pupa-cases wide
and the wings, the lives, have flown.

Church Mice

In the nave and aisles
we roll in holy dust,
bask in the rainbow stains
of sun through glass
and feast on crumbs
of coughcandy,
peppermint and wafer.
We nest in hassocks,
drink from the font
and void in the vestry.
We are blessed by anthems,
cleansed by prayers;
our whiskers whiffle with worship.

Do not fear devils
in the shadows.
The bright bootbutton eyes
beneath the pews,
behind the crosses,
are we we we
breathing God's breath
warm as nutmeg
on His knee.

A cinquain

brown thrush
shattering shells
slick naked snails glisten
for a moment like severed tongues
then sing

City of Departing Angels

They stand on the corners,
opening wings like switchblades.
Underground runs on their eyeballs,
mapped out in blood. The posters scream:
You could feel this too!
Men believe and do not believe.
They pass broken cardboard boxes, too tired
to rummage for that last small gift.

The angels rise and drift
on brownstone thermals. They lick
the neon of movie-house signs, waggle
their bright tongues, but say
nothing. Soon they will break free
from the atmosphere, move up, move off.

Fuck you, one gestures with his tail.
Fuck you because you never fucked us.
You sucked the animals out of us
and left us hollow – glowing husks,
burnt paper bearing shadow words.
You never embraced the lion, the bear, the fox.

You never saw the lynx-tufts on our ears.
So fuck you, you sad forked fuckers
We are off to roll in the fleshmills
of Cygnus and Andromeda
and you can kiss the vapour
of my sweet celestial arse.

The Civet Instructs Her Kits

I will tell you how he forged the wind
from three coins and an eagle's squawl,
and polished it with brine and sunshine.
You wonder where he got the coins?
There were gods abroad then. They walked
among the great black-haired trees;
sometimes they stumbled on the roots.
Their pocket-goods scattered in the bracken
and they were too lofty to forage for what
was lost. But he poked in the debris
of each year and found their droppings.

He was not too proud to stoop, and let that
be a lesson to you – what lies on the ground
may have fallen from the sky. You wish
to know about the eagle? She was the ancient one
who watched the mountains fold up
from the sea-bed, who saw the moon's
first shy approach. Her quills rattled like arrows
in a quiver, her voice hollowed the night.

He saw himself reflected in her golden gaze
without flinching. She opened her beak
and gave him power, a blast of brazen horn.
He held her cry in his hands, and carried it
to the flames for tempering. When he had honed
and launched the fledgling wind, it took
sweet water from the high lakes to moisten
the land. The greening began. The earth
awoke, and he rested by the embers
of his fire, and heard promises scurrying
on small swift feet over the breaking bounds.

a clerihew

When Aphrodite
wore a sexy nightie,
green-eyed Hera
went one sheerer.

Clogs

The Queen Mum's gorn and popped her clogs;
the telly's stuffed with Royal progs.
I've heard a thousand epilogues
now the old Queen Mum has popped her clogs.

The Queen Mum's gorn and popped her clogs
so let's fish out our mourning togs
and toast her name in small eggnogs.
Our dear old Queen Mum's popped her clogs.

The Queen Mum's gorn and popped her clogs.
Oh, Gawd, we'll all go to the dogs,
and princes will turn into frogs
now the old Queen Mum has popped her clogs.

Colonel Blimp Addresses the Troops

We'll send you to a hostile place
and hope that you will serve with grace.
And when you've killed your quota, then
we trust you'll act like gentlemen.

The concubine's charm

It is a silver ball, a sphere
with hammered surface scribed
with curves. It resembles part

of an astrolabe or other star-seekers'
paraphernalia, but it is tiny, designed
to hang from a bracelet. The hollow globe

once opened on a minute hinge, but
now it is sealed. What was inside
he has removed, and what he substituted

she does not know. She shakes
the shackling links around her wrist,
listens to the small sharp ring

and wonders what he chose
to fill a world.

The Consuming Angel

My angel is shaped from clouds, a purl
of dove-feathers, the maidenhead of snow
and sugar crystals, but at the core, an engine

turns and churns and steams to propel
his huge benevolence. White and winged
he trundles down the pavements and into shops,

secreting sides of salmon, brie, sheep's heads,
beneath his robes between blessings. A nun
genuflects in his shadow. He turns and smiles

and O the sun spins from the horizon,
gibbous glory blazes out upon the crowd,
the high street is transfigured. Shoppers weep

into their pockets as he passes by,
trailing tail-stream prayers and sweetness
like the kiss of an old contagion.

A conversation with the dark

So tired of it, you bastard, tired of waiting,
tired of halt-breath time, anticipating
your cloven footfalls on my ribs – so blast
your eyes and ears – it's in my hands at last.
You sit like dust again behind the door.
I yank it wide to seize your hair, and roar,
I have you now! And slighter than I knew.
It was your shadow I had feared, not you.

I grasp you, grip you in my termite jaws,
you pissant prick. I seize you in my claws
and squeeze, you rat-turd, arse-wipe, moldwarp, minge.
The stalker stuck, laddo, too late to whinge.
I've grabbed you, gagged you, so don't try to beg.
Shut your throat and listen: Chicken. Egg.

The Corner Shop

They went on Hajj this year. She was determined.
She said It cost him nearly £20,000, good!
She was heavy with child, and they took the children,

two boys and a girl, who were not impressed.
In one place, Abu says, they had to sleep out in the open,
imagine, not even in tents but on the plain ground.

It was all stony he complains, but somehow the space
where mother spread her mat had no stones.
She said she met her in-laws. They do not like her

and she does not like them. Now they are home,
she is working in the shop again,
heavier with child. It is only weeks now, but

she has not seen a midwife. She did not return
to the doctor's surgery after he told her about the cancer.
She will not have treatment because of the baby.

She serves me with milk, a white loaf and The Times,
then takes a furtive suck at a bottle of Coca-Cola
which we know she should not drink. We smile.

In the street I look up at the veiled stars, and wonder
if she dreams of clear nights above desert places
where a mother sleeps without stones.

The Correspondents' Song

(with apologies to Betjeman)

Come friendly bombs and drop on us –
we'll break or die with little fuss.
We may lose our lives or legs
but waging war involves cracked eggs.

We feel so smart, embedded here,
in our spanking combat gear.
We like to hear our generals' views
for we are pledged to spread the news.

Costanza Carved

Of course, you packed the bloody bust away:
I'm sure your bride preferred to see it go.
Your former love – the scandal – such foul play –
too dark a thing to grace a groom's trousseau.
It's true your deft hands nearly killed your brother,
yet, what man would tolerate that slight,
the horns bestowed fraternally? Your mother
called the guards and spared his hide that night.

And you reformed. A tardy penitent
shaped saints and angels with sweet blessed heads.
Did God forgive the razor that you sent
to slice her perfect, faithless face to shreds?
And did you doubt the glories of your stone
redeemed that living flesh slashed to the bone?

Countdown

Her doctor prescribes calcium tablets
to strengthen bones – a buttress against
the effects of anno domini, the domino

effect of taps turned off tightly,
sluices stemmed, the dying-up
of channels. The white discs, large

as lovehearts, are soft, crumbling
with an after-crunch of chalk.
She thanks something for her own teeth

and sees letters, large figures
on a blackboard, problems set
to ponder quietly while the teacher

leaned back in his chair, and embarked
on Napoleonic seas with Forester.
She can recall the gold braid pressed

into his bookclub covers, the smell
of pale peppermints he used to suck.
As you near the end, the beginning

becomes closer and clearer. When you fold
a letter, Dear Sir and Yrs sincerely
touch. All that remains is the slide

into an envelope and a stamp
for the black expectant slot. Perhaps
a kiss for luck.

Crawlspace

My house has an extra storey,
reached by a narrow trapdoor and tunnel
that involve a twist of body.
There are no windows though a lamp
still burns from an old black
and white film I saw as a child.

The mustard bulb is too dim to light
the corners. I do not like to ascend
to that space but the dark always
twists me in its tale and makes me climb
upstairs. There are people I know well
but would not recognise awake –
night's familiars – they know my secrets
and the weak spots in the floor.

I think about the strait turn down
towards the safety of the lower storeys.
I think tomorrow I will not know
these faces, these fears, but they always
wait for another night nearer the roof,
in the rooms the day destroys.
Sometimes I sit up late, warm china
in my fingers, trying not to listen
as the clock counts up the stairs.

Curves

She hates being the second wife, not that she admits it
with any little line set in her forehead. Once her nurse
held her face so close to a mirror that its meniscus
radiated cold into her skull, saying, Maaijke, Maaijke,
see how the temper-demon turns you into a monkey.
Ecch, by the time you're ready to be married,
they'll put the dress on old Dirk's marmoset instead.
So she learned not to frown, to hold the creases
inside. Now she has many mirrors for reflection

and sometimes she pulls back her thick black hair
to gaze at her smooth forehead. She plucks her eyebrows
into arches, and the shape is like the pain of tweezers
which makes her sneeze. She has learned much
about small paths of pain since she married.
Maaijke, she hears his first wife call, and settles back
into a dusty shadow, soft lips facetting like cut stone.
Her fingers move to her belly, tracing out the curve.
It echoes the arch of her eyebrows. They are her weapons.

Say his first wife proves barren – seventeen moons already
and no fruit. Perhaps soon, she will not be so important.
Perhaps her husband will no longer suddenly stop
speaking when the first wife enters. Maaijke's lips curve
as her fingers curl around the small leather pouch
she wears around her neck. Of course, she is too modern
to believe in obi, but a little black musk, painted beads,
a dome of bone, more like a seashell than the skull
of an unborn monkey – well, it can't hurt. She slides further
behind the shield of the shesham chest, cradling the charms
in one palm, and her belly in the other, listening
to the imperious voice calling out her name. A spider
trails silk from ceiling to wall, blurring the corners.

Cutlet, Mince of Denmark

(A Tragedy in 4 Lamentable Fillets).

Act 1:
What fowl noisette's abroad this night? I walk
the battlements. Porked lightning! Next appears
my father's goose. O Veni, son, he says. We talk
of offal oxtails – poussin in his ears!

Act 2:
I ham a madman's veal. My plans are laid.
I rib Orphelia, my lamb, and swear
that she's croquette and worse, that sweetbread maid.
She drowns, a bouquet garni in her hair.

Act 3:
The barons and the burgers beef. I do not quail.
Words dripping on the tongue, I tell the cast.
I steak my all upon my play. It mutton fail.
I'll pluck my uncle's heart and crown at last.

Epilogue:
The thyme is out of joint, and drumsticks thrum.
Did Bacon write this tripe? The butchers come.

The Dancing Bride

When I was six, and dainty-footed, my parents sold me
to a pedlar, to pay for modern goods they craved:
a washing machine to counsel the neighbours,
two televisions to till the garden, and a computer
that pupped keys to all the doors in the world.
I turned and waved, but they slammed the gate.

The pedlar put me on his tray to dance. I spun
like maple seeds. I whirled into cream, into butter,
my breasts were soft pale curds. I melted
into a salty cracker and swallowed myself.
On the seventh day I rose with clouds in my eyes
and sandalwood nipples. I knew my place
on the mountain. I grew like a princess pine.

Resin sweetened at my core and I threaded calling birds
through my needles. The west wind carried me off and
made me his wife. Lightning sheeted our bridal bed
and thunder rocked it seven times seven that night.
He leaves his feather sandals with me, so I can fly.
When he's abroad, I hear the earth whispering
through the wounds men make. When he returns
I hear nothing but his words. Nothing save his words.

I gathered all the tears my mother never shed
and gave them to my husband. I poured them
into the cup of his hands. He rains them on the village
where I was born, and my small brothers and sisters run
into the yard, and tilt their heads, quick-eyed as robins.
Beware of wolves, I whisper to them, beware of wealth.
But my words are lost above the water's mill.

Daughters

Hadiya
(Arabic: gift)

A pedlar comes to our gate, laden
with goods from the caravan. He has silks,
jewellery, perfumes, spills of spices,
and embroidered rugs and wall-hangings.
He will accept only silver and gold. All our coins
are bronze. The dogs snap at his heels.

Miriam
(Hebrew: rebellious)

My brother bathes in streams that flow
from high pastures. He tints the water red
with the dust of his feet. The birds sing
as he washes his loins. It sounds like a psalm,
but it is a complaint from small thirsty throats.

Xochitl
(Nahuatl: flower)

In this year I will give birth to a child,
who will be named by the priests. His father
was stretched across the altar. I saw
his living heart raw as an abortion. I think life
is hard, but I do not want the gods to know.

Jiao
(Chinese: beautiful)

I work in the flooded fields. Flies surround me
as if I have secrets. I wish I had a robe
as blue as the sky. When I was a child
my mother twisted me a sorrow doll
from wheat stalks. It had black seeds
for eyes. I see it walking in my dreams.

Marysia
(Polish: bitter)

He touches me, his fingers dark with bird's blood.
The fox has been in the run again. Feathers flurry
in the air, stick against the wire, soft as sleep.
That there are no hens and no fox does not matter –
the deed is in his eyes.

Sophia
(Greek: wisdom)

My father's horse is sick. I pull long sweet grass
and meadow flowers for her. I comb her mane
and brush her sides. I gave the wise woman
my birthday bracelet in return for herbs.
Each day the mare is stronger. I wind
my arms around her neck and murmur
into the brown arum of her ear.

The Dead Zone

Il Duce dangling like a hog,
Pol Pot, nose bunged by cotton,
Ceausescu and his wife gunned down –
gone but not forgotten.

Now Saddam's sons are on the news
both whammed, bammed, and well-chastised.
Thank God we learn from history:
we're far more civilised.

Dear Reader

If you chance upon this book,
remember all the pains I took,
and how I sweated day and night
to get these poems sounding right.
If I can't sign this verse with pride,
let it be said, at least I tried –
but shit! Forget it, you're the rotter
who's just dropped in for Harry Potter.

Death Abroad

The phone is ringing late. My stomach tingles
with its tone. Matthew from Brunswick: Hi, Hon,
brace yourself; it's not good news. I slip into a chair
and wait. Kate's remission's ended. It must be that.
Jack died last night. They broke down the door
when he didn't open the store and the phone kept
ringing. It was a heart attack. He went in his sleep.
He didn't suffer. A long pause. It was awkward. Trucks
around the block. It took time to move the books.
They had to get his body on a gurney and hoist him
up the stairs. It's a mess down there. His sister's
coming over later today. I say something, put down
the phone, sit.
                 Jack had lived in the basement
of the bookstore since he came home and hung up
his uniform. He kept the gun. It was a mess down there,
stanchions supporting the upper floor, bare brick walls,
and piles of books. Something about the naked metal
and dust made him feel at home. He pitched a tent
down there and slept on a camp bed. You couldn't see
any war wounds. Jack kept to himself and guarded
the books. He wasn't ill. He went to the local bar
and drank with his pals. He cursed politicians,
pinkos and things in general. He had nightmares
and a disability pension from the government.
He said the country was a mess. He watched TV
a lot. He didn't suffer. I pick up a book from the floor,
replace it on the top shelf, think about sleep.

Death and the Donkey

'Donne's famous piece on Death? Well, naturally,
I know it well, but think my copy's lost.
Perhaps you'll lend me your anthology?'
You briefcased it. Alas, Donne's sonnet crossed
a page, and at the funeral, you rushed
the octave, closed the book, pi-faced – so cruel
to leave that sweet sestet unvoiced. I crushed
the urge to cry out 'Finish it, you fool!'

Resentment rankles still. She was denied
the triumph of that close, and, unashamed,
it seemed Death sniggered in my ear. You lied:
You did not know the poem as you'd claimed.
That night, alone, I read the verse aloud.
Both Death and dolts lack reason to be proud.

Death Replies

Dear Dean, I wonder you should think me proud.
I socialize with all ranks, rich and poor,
and greet the fair and foul, the saint and whore.
I have no side. I celebrate the crowd

and mix with famine, crime and poison cloud.
Life's dregs and cream alike receive my cure,
as free to filthy scum as to the pure.
All strata sift into a common shroud.

I'm hurt that you unjustly look askance
on one who scrupulously smooths and levels,
who takes a downright democratic stance.
Do not confuse me with your haughty devils –
I am the caller of a vulgar dance:
bow to your right, link hands and join my revels.

Death scene

Rehearsing in his head what he will see,
the cop sighs as he walks along the hall.
Another Pollock painted on a wall
with gouts of blood and brains, but mindlessly.
They never think of who must scrub the room,
ignoring cleaner ways to forfeit hope –
the pills and plastic bag, or choke of rope –
and choose the Western way, a graphic boom.

The girlfriend has arrived. Send Gilchrist down
to break the news. He has the tender knack.
Another death to document, more mess,
another final pratfall for a clown.
He stuffs an unsmoked Lite back in its pack,
then breathes and feels the movement in his chest.

December 28

Father, can I see you
about my cat. He's very ill.
I took him to the RSPCA
and got a tapeworm pill

but nothing seems to work,
I'm sure he's getting worse.
Can you suggest a soothing psalm
or helpful Bible verse?

I know God's busy in the clouds
doing stuff and healing crowds.
Is there a moment for my kitty
in the kingdom of His pity?

My kitty can't explain in words
but he doesn't kill the little birds
He stays with me inside my flat
and is a good and gentle cat.

Father forgive me if I'm wrong
but I've loved my kitty for so long.
I've seen small angels in the sky
with fur and whiskers flying by.

Dear Father, if you're not too busy,
please hold my hand and bless my pussy.

(December 28: The Feast of the Holy Innocents)

Demon Lover

I sensed you were a follower of Set –
the way you grumbled at the dawn each day,
kept pipistrelles in pockets, and a pet
with three fierce heads to snarl and bark and bay.
I knew you were a demon when your eyes
went black and something vipered into view.
Of course I felt a soupçon of surprise
but Honey, what the hell, I still loved you.

I scarcely scent the brimstone now, it blends
with violet and lavender so well.
Did human sex transmute your horny glands
or have I lost my dogged sense of smell?
Ah well, no man is perfect and at least,
I'm topped and tailed by beauty and the beast.

Descartes for the 21st Century

Man:
I fart
therefore I am.

Woman:
I shop
therefore I am.

Child:
I ask
therefore I am.

Teenager:
I think
you're pissing me off.

Ding Dong Bell

Great Bast, today she pulled out all the stops,
all faff and fussle to impress her friends;
the bedrooms were a whirl of cloths and mops,
much bathroom bleach sploshed all around the bends,
great waspiness of Hoover on the stairs.
She wore a gypsy scarf to dust and clean,
to brush the suite and tut at velcroed hairs.
I split, aloof, – upheaval's not my scene.
She's donned a dress, a closet lecher's dream,
the pristine kitchen's pregnant with fine food,
the startled rooms and furniture all gleam.
Ding Dong. Her guests arrive in festive mood.
Ah, that's my cue to squat with blissful hiss
and souse the Persian rug with pungent piss.

Drama Class (intermediate)

Cesare claps his hands, declares that today we will be doing horses.
Of course, the whole horse, an e n t i r e equine,
would be too ambitious at this stage, so we will do
a horse in bits: Excuse the Pun!! hah hah hah.
Lilian is a nostril, big and black and slightly steaming,
while Thomas becomes an ear, tall and delicate, softly
pricked towards the window. Jonathan is a hoof, round,
shiny-faced and dependable. Clara turns into tail,
glossy as a hazelnut, rippling against the white wall,
and darling Delphine bends her ballerina spine into a neck.
Naturally Jacob is the prominent eye, quick and brilliant,
while I curl in the corner, rehearsing an archetypal A .

Drawing from Life

Two apples and a peach. The bruised pear
I replaced in the slick Tesco bag,
and the chequered tablecloth I folded
neatly along its pattern.
                        So the fruit
sits on the polished wood, reflecting.
I have pinned a new sheet of paper
to my board with due tautness
and determination. Now I look
                        with proper eyes.
See the colours and curves and the lines
which do not exist. Let the point
of the pencil trace out their relationships,
balance them perfectly in the space
allotted;
            considering, as I think, that one side
of my brain says that this peach is simply
a peach, like any other peach, categorises
and dismisses peach,
                        and
the other side
sees this peach with special grace
so deep and unique that I could lose
myself in peach for hours
            while somewhere
else an urgent hand counts time
like a Dickensian clock, upright
and bewhiskered.
                As I forget to think,
only feel the shapes and hues,
the luscious greens and yellows
blushing into scarlet and vermilion
stripes like the tulips I held years ago,

soot-black pollen on my fingers,
taste of butter on my tongue,
the gold and apricot velvet arcing
against a dim blue plane of wall.

These are only three fruit, says reason,
set out on a board, but intuition
rolls them out like little worlds
and opens wide the gates of Eden.

The Drawing Lesson

Outside the Master's fine stone house,
the chaperone drowses in the grass.
Bees are loud in her ears, the sun
is heavy on her lids. She is not bored
in her solitude: servants love to do nothing.

Inside, the occupants are busy. The Master
is teaching his pupil about perspective, the laws
of diverging lines and the horizon. Horizontal,
he instructs her in other mysteries. She gazes
down between their linked bodies, sees
the foreshortening of loins and dark sex.

On the wall one of the Master's angels hovers
in a cypress frame, the gravity of its face
and wings foreshadowing discovery,
but the day is hot and sweet, alive
with insects. A bell swings and speaks
softly from an ice-grey tower.

The Master kisses her fingers, bronzed
by crayon-dust, whispers that some draughtsmen
insist on the silver pencil. Once it marks the paper,
the line cannot be erased. It instills accuracy
and care, forewarns against error
before the lines are inscribed.

Outside, the servant girl unwraps
a white kerchief of food, a chunk
of fresh bread, crumbling cheese, green figs.
blood-red shining cherries. She feasts,
sighs, drowses again. Ants investigate
the crumbs. A wasp probes a wounded fruit.

Dreaming in the Batmobile

Over Venice, he starts to drowse.
He pictures Giotto's angels
gathered with their hymn sheets,
carolling on golden stairs. Their wings
and open lips follow him into a room
where his old Divinity tutor is discussing
bats, how they fly with their hands,
the skin taut between wide-spread fingers.

A blonde girl whispers, No, the hands
are on the wingtips, look , and he sees
little clusters of digits. So it is with angels:
Professor Bellini intones, they lack arms.
Their radii and phalanges lurk behind plumed flesh.
They must pick up words with their toes,
clawed and curved like mandrake roots.

Coffee? He wakes with a start and is bathed
in the brilliant smile of the stewardess.
He nods and inhales Java fragrance
as she fills a porcelain cup. A brown bead
hovers on the gold rim. He drinks but caffeine
can't stave off sleep, which sweeps under him
deep as the ocean beneath the fuselage.

The bat is on the desk, drawn up into a gargoyle.
Water starts to spew from its mouth, and a technician
leaps forward to close a spigot. The plane drones
into the lecture room, and he glances out of the window
at the smooth arc of wing. The bat squats there, huge.
He thinks of The Twilight Zone, a gremlin chewing
on the engine. He opens his mouth
to yell, but no sound comes. He wakes up
to a yawn, stretched wing-skin taut.

He opens a clutch of ham sandwiches, and chomps
slowly, his eyes prickling with sand. Africa
streams below them. Soon they will land
on a grey field and he will take his suitcase
to a long bungalow thatched with leaves.
Small bats hang there, ready to skim for flies
in the twilight. Evie says they harbour fleas,
but he's never been bitten. The flies,
on the other hand, suck every night. He rubs
his chin, feeling ghost bristles, closes his eyes.

The lecture is over, and the blonde, who
becomes Evie, leans over to copy his notes.
He untucks a pipistrelle from his breast pocket,
strokes its soft fur, then casts it up through
an open skylight, into the clouds
where the plane is circling, descending
to the wide bright land, his home.

Drips from Psyche's Lamp

Tell me you're blind at night and I'll believe you.
Tell me they raise the sky on ten thousand turquoise poles
and I won't quibble. I'll point out the flapping canopy,
and the places in the T-shirt clouds where their points stand out
like nipples. I don't care about lies, about tall tales,
only about the tourniquet musk of you, the bowstring tight
around my aorta so my brain pulses harder than my heart,
all thoughts turned to sparkles.

                      Wind me in your elastic
time so I'll live forever before breakfast, so I'll fall apart
and curl in a yolk, then break out all gold and new
like a Paschal chick on a daffodil cake. Launch me
on a crocus sea. I don't care if you're blind at night,
if the sky collapses on me like a marquee in a squall.
I'll be ova, ovine, big sheep's eyes,
I'll be nova, novacodeine, noddy as a noodle,
I'll be tangy, tangerine, mango, mandarin,
tango, tanga, bingo bongo bang.

The Drowning Gypsy

Flamboyant
Clairvoyant
Unbuo
o
o
o
o
y
a
n
t

The Duke A-Hunting

("E'en then would be some stooping" –Robert Browning)

Today we step out for his sport and pleasure
across the wide estate, trout-streamed and wooded.
The Duke calls for his pets, his feathered treasure,
and cadge-boys bring the birds, gold-belled and hooded.
My lord extends his leathered arm, his eyes
as bright as gold-clasped gems that stud his fist.
He scans a perch and picks the sleekest prize,
a full-summed peregrine to grace his wrist.

She cuts the morning wind, a grey-fletched arrow
dispatched to strike the prey. She stoops, kills cleanly,
then mantles jealous wings to claim the sparrow.
A merlin stirs and snites. He eyes it keenly.
"Hush, sweetheart, hush," he whispers, maiden-mild,
and strokes it like rich silk, a coin, a child.

The Dying of the Day

Above his head the helicopter blades
beat like a palpitating heart. He sees
veridian and emerald, deep shades,
ribbed jungle crouching, leopard-lithe, as trees
arch down to glinting sea, with boats like toys,
so clear and close, he could stretch out his hand
and touch the bobbing gulls, the warning buoys,
dwarf waves that wash a miniature bright land,
and further out grey slippers of great ships
with friendly guns and sailor dolls for crews,
before the blue-green plane side-slips and dips
in dreams, a fading pulse through fevered hues.
The wound from slanting steel still bleeds, still bleeds;
the flight of sun is done. The light recedes.

Ego

A shamanistic friend tells me solemnly
about his astral journeys, of the passage
through the ether that is not empty, but alive
with golden energetic swirls, sparkling
like dust-motes in shafts of sunlight,
about his speakings with the spirits of animals,
that they have souls untainted by ego, unlike humans.

I think of a blackbird fluting variations of MemeMe
into the growing dawn, the stallion coralling his kingdom,
sly squirrels rolling requisitioned nuts like Sisyphus,
the jealous cat who shoulders his brother aside
to usurp a caress, his gaze twin 'I's in amber –
but I nod. We all have our truths, our knowledge.
Why shake the fruit from another's tree?

Egypt

I am dying, Egypt, dying
and all the weight of night
and Nile is on my shoulders
and my brow. The helmet
breached, the armour cracked
open like a wounded turtle
the carapace of jewels
is scattered on the flood-plain.

I am dying, Egypt, dying.
The constellations whirl
children's tops whipped
singing like green crickets
the lilies droop, the lotus
lifts his heavy head no more
armies retreat, blinded
by battle and Ra's brazen gaze.

I am dying, Egypt, dying
and Rome sinks into darkness
the age of heroes ends
as Antony paints the desert
with his blood. Ice and metal
seal the sorry future
the heat and passion drained.

I am dying, Egypt, dying
cold Augustus will calculate
the cost in columns
our defeat his triumph
our bloody loss his profit
he will grey the world
and bleach the coinage
we die without glory

but glory dies with us
look, my love, in the East
the brightness fades.

Elaine: suicide bomber

But Lancelot mused a little space.
He said, "She had a lovely face
before she spread it every place.
The Lady of Shalott.

The Elements

There is a point in the sea-swell
of together when the keel grates
against an island. Perhaps if we had hired
a more experienced navigator
we would have avoided this sudden grounding,
but the pilot we chose was more interested in air
than water. He would rather flirt with the stars
than calculate precise positions.

I had a steely sextant once,
but he dropped it
into the moon's reflected gaze
when we passed though the Azores;
he pleated the charts into planes
and lanterns, feathered my pens for darts.
Now I must light a fire to melt pitch
and you can hammer at necessities.
We will re-launch into a fair wind.

Later we may discover
a small winged stowaway
bright-eyed amongst the ropes and canvas.
Do not scold him. Lift him into the arms
of Zephyr and let him fly
over trade-routes, trails and dragons
into the wide uncompassed day.

Emily abandons her breasts

Emily felt an old brass ring tightening
around her finger, heard links creak
around her strait waist, tight as family;
and saw the circle of lamplight
squeezed smaller and smaller
as she squinched her eyes to read
the notes perched on her small piano.

She clung to that, her rosewood raft,
like a stowaway suddenly wrecked
without ever strolling through the ship
to enjoy the starched napkins,
the monogrammed cutlery and crystal,
the curliques upon the menu.
Emily feared she would be rolled up
like bills in a man's pocket
amongst the must and fust
and fingered things.

One night, she unlaces her stays
for the final time and scratches
her latticed skin luxuriously.
Everything falls away easily, the skirts,
the petticoat, earrings, necklace, name.
Only her long hair bleeds a little
as she sheds it. She dresses in shirt
and britches, folds her future
into a carpet-bag, and quits the Old World
for the salt of the New, her small breasts
bound flat, but not with whalebone,
her face buoyed by decision.

One day she will uncurl like camellia petals
but now, she furls into hard green bud,
throwing thorns over her shoulders.
Out on to the lawn and the moon's fresh O.
Sister, fare well, but never farewell,
for her rise will be your music and her pale face
the ivory of keys.

Europa

When I first came to the paddock bar,
I felt the hot breath, heard a bellows
of leathern lungs, damp as wineskins,
saw those eyes, deep and dark like night
reflected in a lake. I was an ivory doll,
a votive carving thrown open-mouthed,
into the pool of iris.

O, I ran. My garments whipped around me
like an angry tutor's tongue. I flew
into the fields and panted, one hand
against my ribs, pressing my pulse,
a bird in bone-cage.

Then I forgot, until that day it stood
before me on the beach, scattering sea
from its shaggy coat. My fear drove me
forward. I mounted the broad back,
dug my naked heels into pelt and muscle,
felt the surge of movement, rode power
into the creaming surf.

The wind laced brine into my locks, the gulls
keened, the sun raced beside me. My heart
was bursting with light and life. On the far shore
I met the fullness of myself, my breasts, my loins,
the liquids of my body as I slid beneath his belly
to the ground. The land was mine, seeded by sun
and salt. I saw markets, temples, towers, armies,
libraries,cities – furled on a scroll, unreeling
in flesh and fire and gold.

The Exchange

The telephone is intimate at times
but still remote. I did not want bad news
transmitted by attenuated lines.
I need a human interface. I'd choose
proximity of warmth, the flesh in phase
to press. Instead I dropped the phone and bled
inside, alone and shoulderless, no gaze
to mirror grief, so tears were left unshed.
You spoke of time, about a given span,
a term of months, despite your former hope
prognosticated from the prod and scan.
Now truth's a stain beneath a microscope.
It starts with one rogue code, a single glitch –
branches cross, clump, till they pull the switch.

Expectations

Estella buried Pip
in the blasted graveyard
where the convict found him
long ago.

He died of a cracked heart.
She lays a maroon rose
on the gravel mound
and smiles.

Did you, my dear,
believe in happy endings?
She keeps her wedding gown
wrapped with camphor
in case.

The Ex-Romantic

with apologies to E.B.B.

How do I hate you? Let me count the ways:
I hate you from the bottom of my bowels,
and from the height of mind's disdain, with blaze
of bile, and with the throat's disgusted howls.
I hate whole-hog. I hate your stubbly jowls,
your farts, your lies, your smirks, the way you laze
while I wash up, the way you drop damp towels.
I hate you faithfully through all our days.

I live in hope you'll be an early croaker;
a Matterhorn of fat may cause a stroke, a
Windermere of beer may choke a joker.
A light? Thank God you're such a heavy smoker.
One day in hell your fire may need a stoker –
I'll be one busy devil with the poker.

The Eyelids of Langerhans

A scan reveals landscapes. Tribes move
and settle across the browns and greens,
stand on the rim and gaze over the ocean.

Where the peoples gather, there is blood-orange,
breath-warmth, flues of body-furnace seeking sky.
Strange migrations up and down slopes, following rain.

Drum and thrum of industry, turning, transformation. Trade
on winds. The changes squeeze the heart, adrenalin tides
scour raw shores. We are afraid of parasites.

They leech on our nerves. We disown them.
But populations breed, new nations rise.
Their flags are flying in the interstices

between thoughts. They ford the synapses. They name
our organs, brand our parts. They will sell us, joint
by joint, in their tents and dog-eared markets.

Eye rhyme

I'll clone myself. I've got the DNA.
The techie side, I'm sure, will be a breeze.
I'll surf the shelves for tomes to teach the way;
a first-aid course will hone my expertise.
A scrape of cells, some needlework (I'll cope.
I once grew cress upon an dampened cloth),
some gel, some slides, a shop-soiled microscope,
a jolt of juice to start mitosis off.

There'll be no nasty natal blood and screams.
Each birth will be immaculate. I'll sow
me in glass beds and monitor my dreams,
build up my strength with patent BayBee-Gro.

I've studied this sad world; we need to breed
and broadcast mes, before it goes to seed.

Fairytale

Did you ever believe that
the wolf ate Grandma?
She'd have told him off,
polished his personal buttons
with a spit-damp hankie,
sat him down at a white tablecloth
and fed him homemade scones,
seedy jam and Madeira sponge.
Do you remember the twisting swirl
of lemon peel on the top
like a magical symbol, gold and soft?
She'd have pinched his cheeks and
rumpled his hair mercilessly, asked
if he had clean underwear.
"In case of an accident, dear."
O, many times worse than being mangled,
the shame of dirty undies
laid bare before a medical team.
She'd tell him how big he'd grown
and Watch Out for the china lady ....
Big Bad Wolf? Hah!
He'd slope out, sheepish.

Falling

In the library,
you fell over me.
You said, So sorry.
I said, Ouch.
Later you fell over me
on the couch.

Things were falling into place,
thigh to thigh and face to face.
Earth was falling
through the night
falling into birds and light.

As the sky unrolled
another day,
you kissed me,
then you walked away.

But walking,
I'm told,
is merely
falling
controlled.

Family Feeling

So Bobby has the case. The trouble is
it's not his case. Who did the switcheroo
and when? On Bob – my tricky dick, a Wiz
who fixed scores coast to golden coast – and who
could match his balls, who beelined all the biz?
So I can't trust him now? My number 2.
Sweet Jeez, we had it stitched, the fuse had fizz
but now the nose-cone's in the shit. What's new?

Tell Bob to buzz his butt. He's got one day
to find the green, to close this tight. If not,
I'll treat the seagulls to a fresh buffet –
Capeesh? That bastard's costing me a lot.

Hey, Bob has found the case? The deal's all done?
That Bobby boy, I love him like a son.

Fer Blossom

Tha's not allowed ta bury pigs, tha knows.
I blinks et Blossom's bulk stratched awt on
a bad of bettercups end pink-tinged deisies,
ayes closed es ef ha nipped off en a nep.
Ha ware a soft awd boy. Et ferst ha wouldna touch
tha sows, naver mend thet thay becked partly et him,
but once ha got tha heng of et, ha did his duty
like tha bast. Ha used ta stend nose t'nose
with em grunting softly aftwards. Thare ware summack
about Blossom, but now ha's deed. Deed waight.

Ha'll hefta be hautopsied end cinerated. Hup
en a cloud of smoke. Ha ware naver dastined
fer becon. Ha ware a pat. Ferst I kneels down
ta buss his ear. Farewall Blossom. This es ow
I'll ramember tha, mettressed on meadow,
paceable. I hopes thay'll rub tha stummack
end stroke tha snout, jest es tha liked.
I hopes thay'll know tha loved persnips,
epples and Meltasers. I knows I'll see
tha trotting up fer tha feed with th'others
tamorrow, but tha won't be thare. I won't
stey fer tha rast of et. Wa both knows thet
don't metter a smutter. Goodbay, Blossom.
Goodbay, awd berrel-bottom boar.

Firstborn

The Fetch farm wife keeps half a field of bees
while, to the west, sweet almond blossoms thrive
like summer snow on John Farr's treasured trees,

and bees lurch down our lawn just half-alive,
exhausted by the journey from the hive.
Conn mixes sugar water in a polished glass
and solemnly he carries it across the grass
to feed the insects from his 'postle spoon.
They fan their wings, and softly rise to croon
about his head before their homeward run.
The priest came round hot, cross, an Easter bun,

to warn the lad was falling far behind
in Sabbath school. But I thought: Hell, my son
knows more of God than all your black-clad kind.

First time father

Just before Janice had the kid
she got very salty.
She'd lie there on the bed
like one of those bull sealions
collecting their harems
on David Attenborough,
and she'd give me the wide eye.

I'd start to sweat cobs
and I couldn't get it up.
I told her it was because
I was worried about crushing the baby,
but it wasn't so much that –
or the swollen slope of her,
with a roadmap of Manchester
all done in purple veins –

it was the thought of the little sod
sticking out his hand and grabbing
hold of my dick. I thought
of the ambulance sirening us
to the General, all three of us
locked together. We'd land up
on the front page of The Echo,
for all the lads to laugh at.

As it turned out,
Janice had a little girl.
When I first saw her
she was the colour of one
of those pink sugar mice
in the posh Belgian chocolate shop,

I have to check on her every morning
to see she's all right
and that I didn't dream her.

The First Woman

As Lilith prowls her realm, the night yields stars
to settle in her hair like sleepy bees,
and by their light, she counts the latest scars
gouged in the planet's pelt by human greed.
A leopardess, she glows and stalks, and feeds
the generation of her fine fierce line.
She laughs at dusty sacred scrolls and screeds.
Who wrote those tales, but spiteful men who lied?

She couched with Adam first, before soft Eve,
and she desired equality, forbidden
by that stern Word which cast her out to grieve
in wilderness – but Lilith made new Eden.
She tore the fruit, then tongued its bitter pips,
and spewed the world's sweet forests from her lips.

Five cans of catfood

Five cans of catfood on a kitchen shelf:
I know soon I must move them out of view.
Are they a hopeful message to myself
that nothing's changed, that time turns tail for you?
No need to cut a jagged tear in tin.
No look that says 'Beef chunks? I fancied ham.'
No need to scrape the lot into the bin;
just pristine labels: Pilchard, Turkey, Lamb.

I sense an empty space upon the stairs.
I feel the unfilled hollow on my bed,
a pang that pounces, takes me unawares,
the silenced mews that prowl inside my head.

Five tins of catfood sealed and set apart,
and ah, a ragged fissure in my heart.

five fingers

Lord, they say I have one soul
can that be right?
perhaps I am made wrong
for I feel many things in me.

most, says my grandmother,
I resemble a monkey;
that is when I chatter
and play and do not listen.

sometimes, my brothers tell me,
I am like a brown deer,
when I run fast, so fast
like the wind stroking spring grass.

then there is the owl of me,
Lord, – my eyes round
with looking and stories
and things to be understood.

stripped for the water,
I become fish, not thinking
or considering, but warm
in the river's fist, forgetting.

when I stand under the stars
there is something more,
a sharp brightness
on tiptoe like a spindle.

when you take one, Lord,
do not leave the others pining,
it is one hand, five fingers.

monkey will ride deer
owl will sail salmon
and light will guide us home.

For Earth: Christmas 2002

Looking on the world at large,
I flinch to think of who's in charge.
Rich, myopic, full of spite,
they claim to represent the Right.
O Sacred Muse, inspire my song –
a plea, a paean, for the Wrong.

For Sarah

Skintight and shiny, that's the fashion now.
Her made-up face reflects the stickered glass
and watched by posters of her passion – Wow,
he's BAD! – she stacks her feet and smooths her arse.
A model Sarah struts a schoolgirl's room,
a painted lady, sweet thirteen. Let's see...
sprays tender tits and thighs with musk perfume,
checks sequined bag for phone and pack of three.

She's off to Cats to meet her mirror mates
in Trance mixed deep and loud, no need to think:
just laugh and dance till timeless night gyrates,
a carousel of music, pills and drink.

When Sarah's shagged across a stranger's bonnet,
She'll never give a fuck for this dumb sonnet.

For Spike Milligan

Ah, Spike, for prince or goon,
Death always knocks too soon.
I know you struggled with the dark
but through the glooms, the spark
of genius was always there
to blaze into a comic flare.
Good luck, old lad, in what comes after,
for now I mourn you with fond laughter.

For the fallen

After the day,
they wouldn't show
the falling ones
on American television;
something about not showing
people near the instant of death.
Something more
about the giving up
on life, a dereliction
of hope, while rescuers
struggled up towards them
through smoke and fire.

I watched it all that day
beamed across the Atlantic,
and those images remain –
stronger than the belch
of flame. The collapsing
fabric of reality –
the individual drops of flesh
with my guts lurching
in empathy.

A digression, perhaps:
A man took a photograph
of people clinging to a ledge.
He didn't blow it up until
people begged him to do it.
They wanted to see.
They didn't want their feelings
spared. They had enough feeling
to spare. They wanted to know
everything.

Now we know
that the fallen did not jump,
that they were thrown off
by fire, blown off by blast.
Does it make the thought
of their falling easier to bear –
that they did not
willingly embrace the air?

The Four-eyed Git Addresses Poets

I wish you would not write poems On Poetry,
particularly about your Poems and Poetry. I find
myself blushing for you, fidgeting in my reading chair,
adjusting my poem glasses because sweat has pooled

beneath the rims. I have to blink – it is Moi mist
that fogs the ground plastic. My literary lenses flinch
like a lemoned oyster. Write about anything, Dear Author,
except Poetry. Adopt any tone, except the self-reverential,

except melting appreciation of your poethead & poethood,
narcissusness reflected in your own words. Echo. Ecce.
Don't wallow in your ultra-sensibility. Swallow your primp
and pomp. Watch a rolled cat – how it spreads its back legs

and licks its arse with a rough fastidious tongue, without self-
conscious spittle. Watch the busy little digits of monkeys
delving in their nether fur. It is not my place to draw
comparisons. I threw away my mirrors years ago.

Frontispiece

With a stroke of blue, a stroke of green
I'll paint an archetypal scene.
Above, deep sky; below, sweet grass
where deer and cattle softly pass.
A brush of brown becomes an oak;
a squirrel lives with one red stroke.
I'll build a house with turtle grey,
white fences to keep fears away,
and in the garden, rainbow shades
of flowers, shrubs and singing glades,
with blossoms, butterflies and birds
more beautiful than any words;
this is my page, this is my art,
this the unlocking of my heart.

Garden birds

I

A wren outside my window
preens in the glossy rhododendron leaves
then spills a line of liquid slip slip notes
three times too large for her frame.
Light as air, brown as earth,
she challenges the winter sky.
Jaunty-tailed, quick, and brave,
she does not know her size
or count the dangers in the grass.

II

A song-thrush surmounts the birch.
Bare of leaves, the tree shines
its bark into the grey day.
The thrush is singing fiercely, sweetly,
claiming branches and bark,
and the orb of heavy sun,
claiming silver and gold, marking all
as his own, his own, wrapped
in the strands of a high strong web.

gateway

he hoped that she would ask him
in but she stands behind the gate
and chats softly, asks about
the postman, was he late, has
he called? she is going out
again, will not return until
the day after tomorrow, would
he take in a package if it came?
he stands beside the gate and
nods, of course, anything, after all,
that's what a neighbour's for,
and she smiles, goes down her path
past mounds of brightfaced violas,
and shuts the slick red door
behind her.

The Ghost of Icarus

The old man sits alone again tonight
and watches as the dark, dazed hawkmoths steer
towards his oil-lamp's spindled flame. They veer
in tightening circles angled to the light,
as once the sun was quartered in their sight.
They still believe they navigate earth's sphere,
but micro- mocks the macro-cosm here
and instinct dooms them to their final flight.

But know, my father, know – I flew at will.
Apollo touched my soul; I heard his voice
and climbed to golden bliss. I fell through choice,
and grasped what poets reach for, quill by quill.
As young men will, I died, still free, aflame,
and spurned some shadowed future, clipped and tame.

Gone before

Please don't think I'll laugh. I've been there too;
grief makes us clutch at straws. I numbed my bum
on creaky chapel chair and New Age pew,
my ears awash with Sacred Muzak, dumb
before a knot of knowing boys and girls
pop-eyed with higher thoughts, the psychic crew
attuned to other planes, dispensing pearls
of comfort for the hopeful, faithful, few.

One night, as I looked round a dingy hall –
torn posters for a talk on UFOs,
a verse from Rumi on the eastern wall,
the fey clairvoyant spouting fuchsia prose –
my mother muttered, from some inner space,
'You wouldn't catch me dead in this damn place.'

Grain

I think of Hulme
who fell in Flanders field
like a bloody cliche

and left a small legacy
his testament
to be distributed like bread

his grain fed many tongues
seeded many minds
engendered subtle songs

he hated the facile
despised metre
sought the fresh connection

I wrote this poem
because I want you
to think of Hulme

Gran and the bedbugs

Gran told me that she stayed
with his parents in Wales
for her honeymoon. Bedbugs
marched across the ceiling
in battalions and he stood
on the bed and reached up
to crush them with his bare hands.
She can still remember the smell,
sharp and sweet like death
dissolved in raspberry juice.

Next day, Granda went to Sirhowy
to help his brother build a wall
and the carter came by.
Gran rode with him to town.
On the way she took the reins
and drove the trap and he laughed
at a city girl going so fast.
It was good with the mountain wind
in her face, Gran said,
and green fields slipping by.

There were more sheep than people
and all wandering about.
Gran hoped they wouldn't get run
over. Sometimes she spoke
to them and they looked at her
quite mild and friendy-like.
From the hills she could look
down into the valley and see
the dark mist of the mine.
There were sounds like thunder
but she didn't know if they came
from the sky or the earth.

After the honeymoon
they came back to London
and Gran was glad to leave
the bedbugs, though she missed
the mountains. She often
went to Regent's park to feed
the ducks or to Greenwich
where the squirrels would sit on
your shoulder or pickpocket
the nuts from your coat.

A few months later she heard
Granda's brother had been killed
when the tunnel caved in.
It took a day to dig his body out.
Gran shivered and bagged
all the sheets for the bath-house
to give them a good wash.

She borrowed a bag of laundry blue
from Lil, who had a new baby
with a purple stain on his cheek.
Lil said it was because he was conceived
when she was on. Gran didn't like
to talk about things like that.
She just said she was sure
the mark would fade in time.

Great heart

When your great heart
ceased beating, I think
there was a silence
in the sky, a long echo
of the pulse suspended,
and then a circled sigh
of termination from
the stars and spheres.

When your great heart
ceased beating, I think
there was a shadow
in the spectrum, a fading
of peacock falls and flowers,
a dimming of all colours
as if nature's palette
ran with sullen tears.

When your great heart
ceased beating, I think
there was a fragrance
in the air, of precious attar
burning, of frankincense
and rosewood fuming
from a pyre of dreams.

When your great heart
ceased beating, I know
there was an emptiness.
A grey and sudden chamber
opened in the tower
with a sampler spelling
Nothing is as certain
as it seems.

Grey imp

The grey imp on my shoulder
 is full of winter things
Sometimes he is like a stone
and sometimes he grows wings

The grey imp on my shoulder
may jump into your lap
He'll stain your skin and clothing
he's such a sticky chap

The grey imp on my shoulder
has been with me for years
I feed him on my sorrow
and quench him with my tears.

Grounding

When the hull grated against an island,
we both cursed crossings, hot-breathed
as buccaneers. The startled parrots flapped
and flakked. A wiser, worldlier pilot

would have avoided this sad scrape,
but our navigator thought more
of air than water. Instead of calculating
angles, he was flirting with the stars.

I saw him drop my steely sextant
into the moon's reflected gaze
when we passed through the Azores.
He pleated sea-charts into butterflies

and lanterns, and played darts
with the dividers. Well, I will light
a fire on the beach to melt pitch,
and caulk timbers, while you hammer

at necessities. We will re-launch
into a fair wind. Later we may discover
a small winged stowaway, bright-eyed,
amongst the ropes and canvas.

Do not scold him. Lift him gently
into the arms of Zephyr and let him fly
over trade-routes, trails and dragons
into the wide uncompassed day.

Growing up with animals

(Adults are prone to create myths about the meaning of adolescence.
– Louise J. Kaplan)

I was an awkward child, always asking
questions, always wanting to know
more: what, if, how, when, where?

Why? my cat reprimanded me silently,
plump on the pillow where she should not be.
She slanted sloe irises at me, signalled

she knew more than I would ever know.
Licking her paw, she viewed the lippy kid
with well-fed tolerance. I was allowed

to stroke the bright plateau of her belly,
caress the tender ears, feel drowsy throbbing
in my lap. The dog waited for me to explain

things. Cats will eat what they need,
then leave the dish. A dog will clear each plate
in case it's never refilled. Seek serenity,

said the furred coil of felinity warming
my thighs, while the spaniel frowned and gazed
across the room at stomach pangs.

Cat and dog brush against each other,
sleep side by side by certain accidents,
breathe in unison through separate dreams.

Gut Reaction

Red in the bowl again, bright shocking spots,
beads strung with spittle, ruby mixed with jet.
Say it's tomato, peppers – there are lots
of explanations for those blobs. Don't sweat.
Just wipe your mouth and fill a steady glass.
The cold tap foams. The water chills your tongue
and shocks your teeth. Grip this new day. Hold fast.
Remember how you felt once, fit and young
before this aged you, greyed your face and bowed
you down, an acolyte of pain, to retch
and spew. For now, no grumbling is allowed.
Stiff upper lip. Don't wimp or whinge. Don't kvetch.
Wait till the angels lift you up, then yell
'Please drop my bloody stomach off in Hell.'

Haemorrhage

She was always a good little girl.
playing with dolls and sewing their clothes.
She baked small cakes, brewed tiny tea.

She loved books about knights and fairies
about princesses in sugarcrust towers,
the good living happily on the last page.

She grew through life in soft fabric
and pastel shades. Her lips were pink.
She married and bore noisy children.

She began to frown even as she smiled.
She managed, she cooked and cared
and ignored her husband's business trips.

Her home was like a hotel, where she paid
the fees. She was always accommodating.
She was sure that loving assured love.

One day her mouth flooded with blood.
It did not come from her teeth or her
throat, but from the chambers of her heart.

Haiku blues

watercolour scenes
paper shines through pastel tints
Alas for my oils

Hairy Story

Possessing prehensile toes, I can understand
large monkeys, their handiness, their problems
in wielding a pen. My feet are small. Faced

with a drill, I could offer up a foot to shake.
However, knowing primates, I think it would prefer
to search my pubic hair for grains of salt.

If this happens, I'm unsure what to do
with my hands. Semaphoring for a keeper
might send the wrong signal. Perhaps

I should stick to orangs. The mandarin male
always slides an arm around my shoulders,
hugs me, titan-tight. He'll snuff the coconut oil

in my curls and suck my cuticles like lollipops.

Here you lie

Here you lie, framed by lilies.
Here you lie embalmed.
Tears gusted around you
but nothing moves the hull
they laid you in, like a warrior
on the last longship, waiting
for the departing tide.

Here you lie, quiet at last,
while they chatter and drink
around you. If it were not
for rigor, your mouth would
turn down at the lack of liquor
in your hand. Well, I'll pour
one for you, Jack, and drink
deep. Here's to you, my friend.

I was with you when the light
faded, when the pain passed
into stillness. They bustled you
away, shouldered me aside,
busy uniforms carrying off
a corpse. I stayed with you, Jack,
by your desk, your monitor,
where a bright blue screensaver
stuck out its cyber-tits.

Here's to you, Jack, old chum.
and I can see your spirit,
raising the single blend
to toast the best and worst times,
and saying 'Fuck them all'.

Hippolyta on a Field of Linen

I sit between his thighs and mark the length
of spine which lifts his head high over mine.
I note his sculptured ribs, his supple strength,
the upright bearing of a martial line.
I broach his shoulder-slope, a neutral zone,
meet no resistance, so press on. My fingertips
are pioneers which take the bridge of bone,
a vanguard reinforced at once by lips.

He sighs, he yields – this skirmish ends too soon –
and he sleeps like one slain, force spent for now,
but I'll engage a battle royal by noon.
They say an army marches on its belly – how
I plan to feast! The world and its alarms
fade, fail, before this morning call to arms.

Holes in the News

They put me in a hole and left me
there. You know the hole I mean.
You scour it out each day until
your armpits leak and blood smears
plum across your nose. When I try
to sleep, they megaphone me, pelt
me with pellets of news. You know
the news I mean.

And I know the other holes
where bodies lie, wrapped or bare,
over-wept or dry. They rot away,
but are replaced. Their faces merge
to one, its mouth becomes black sun.
You know the face I mean. Once

forests filled the holes with roots,
grave leaves rained down. Now
trees are felled for news.
On your knees, you worry at it,
dunk your arms to the elbow in suds,
scrub. You know the brush I mean.

There's a new hole scraped for you.
Wipe your forehead with your wrist.
Rest. What was whole is lost.
You know the rest. I mean once
the forests filled. Faces felled
like trees. Like rain.

Horology as a speculative science

Unfortunately the big ash clock in the hall strikes
Fuck you! on the hour. At noon and midnight,
it indulges in a carillon of cusses, glancing
slyly between its gilt hands, although there
is nothing reticent about its face, bedecked
with sun and moon and planets, a flat
blue astrolabe, smilingly sure of its spheres
and orbits. And if there is no music here,

merely abuse to greet unwary visitors and
embarrass the family, at least it stands square
on four fat feet. From its nature, I can envisage
the timesmith, who was skilled in his craft,
and kept an eye on the heavens as if they were
his concern. The precise nature of his curse
must be surmised, but I feel it was nothing personal,
and the care evident in the wheels, springs and
gearing sings out like a bird full of grasshoppers.

He ensured the hours would be well measured
and designed the case for centuries. Sometimes
I can forget the Fuck you! and think only
of the deft fingers shaping and assembling
and adjusting, to make all sound. There is a name
beneath the clock, but it is difficult to decipher.
Perhaps years blurred it, or the maker rubbed it
away, reluctant to acknowledge the fallibility
of his work. I suspect he has made better.

The horseman

Her eyes are bleached by disappointment;
the years have been unkind.
She brushes down her oatmeal skirt

and checks her lipstick in the mirror,
careful not to meet her gaze.
She saw a film once, years ago,

when her irises were deep with hope,
where death was a cloaked rider
mounted on a great black steed.

Now she is afraid she will open the door
not to a horseman but to empty dark,
and a snort of hoarse laughter –

no steam from a stallion's nostrils.
She looks at the world wearily, warily,
expecting geese to say boo

and swans to duck like addled eggs.

The Host of Darius

You, who were a soldier
in Darius's army
unlock the links of armour
soft clash of surrendered metal
plate by plate
let it fall to the carpets
of the enemy tent

sword unedged by skin
as white as the milk
that froths from mountain heifer
brand unbladed
you are a captive
of alien colours
snared in silks

you who marched in splendour
kneel now
your tongue silenced
by musk and honey
small fingers thread
the spindle of your head
and skein your thoughts
like wool

felled by the rising
of your blood
by the stroke of strings
by the song
in the snailshell flesh
you who were a hero
in the host of Darius

How things change

Things were always quiet round here.
Last excitement was back
when that black dog bit
a neighbour's sow.
Now the air feels darker.

Yesterday, I was browsing
the general store when
two men came in
to buy worms.
They were strangers,
polite, Middle Eastern,
smart business suits.

Sure didn't look like any
fishing-men I'd ever seen,
They started asking questions
about access to the aqueduct.
Hell, that supplies
the whole area with water.

I went home with it
in my head, thought a bit then
picked up the phone.
Felt kinda strange asking for the FBI,
expect they hear from a lot
of nuts these days,
but knew I had to report
what I'd seen and heard.

Seems like we've all moved
closer to the front line
since it happened.

If the ocean is like light

both wave and particle, if salmon leap from turquoise point
to pixel, if a ship lifts its skirts and walks water stone by stone,
if gannets dive into the centre and unearth dragons, if a shark
draws lines from prey to pity, if shells siphon depths to shallows,

if nothing is as it seems, and darkness is vision
if possibility is the fount and foundation
if beginning swallows end
if light is like sea
if light again

In Foreign Fields

Crossed out in white, unwilling,
in tidy ranks we lie.
A few had mastered killing,
but it takes no skill to die.

Like poppy petals spilling,
we fell beneath this sky.
So young men earn their shilling
and the living pass us by.

in hell

in hell they turned me inside out
scraped my guts with strigils
scrimshawed from yellow horn
festooned the ceiling with
ribbon loops of ileum
swags of duodenum swaying
in the dry red breath of furnace

the orbits of my eyes
pierced for shiny gewgaws
my tongue tallowed
for a solitary flame
demons sucked my brains
like oyster, live and moist

on the walls the roadlines
of my bared nerves mapped
the kingdom of my pain
my flesh was transfigured
by cauldron rites and curses

now
you think
you can hurt me?
serpents are secreted in my smile

Internal Memo

Dear Stomach,
                Look, we've really had enough.
Your job is simply to digest the stuff
supplied by Hands and Tongue, to move it through,
not chuck it up. Spurned food is déjà vu
and hurts Oesophagus; she's frankly pissed,
and Face says please forget The Exorcist,
because projectile vomits are not fun
and bloody heartburn hacks off everyone.
Lungs say they're worried by a niggling cough
and Guts say if you won't perform: Sod off!
That's not my phrase–I'm mediating here,
but want to stress the general atmosphere.

Please see these hiccups don't occur again.
I sign myself, sincerely,
                      Upper Brain.

In the translation

Professor Lieberman
spreads his hands,
shrugs, smiles, picks up
a Sobranie, fingers
marinated in mahogany,
inclines his head, pauses,
suckles the black tube luxuriously.

'The Commandments' he announces,
voice thick with tar and the old tongue,
'Yes. There is much of interest here.
Much that puzzles is often
a matter of poor translation.
You understand? Of course you do.
I say sometimes the bone is there
but the meat is lacking.
The flavour has escaped.'

A slow crocodilian smile.
'The stark injunction:
Thou shalt not kill.
No use to vegetarians, I fear.
We will have to argue cause.'
A soft laugh or a cough.
'because the correct translation
would be murder rather than kill.
We are in the sphere
of strictly human interaction,

and, taking it in context,
I would rather express it thus;
Thou shalt not unlawfully kill
another Hebrew. That is my version
of the bone and the flesh
and the flavour. A more complex version
than is generally accepted, you understand.
The translator often seizes simplicity
But what is simple? Life is not simple.'

He reflects and sighs.
Professor Lieberman gestures,
snowing cigarette ash
on to the faded Turkey carpet.
and sighs. On the walls,
dim photographs of his family,
solemnly posed before old brick
and stone, long lost,
sifted in the ashes.

Suddenly he throws off his age
like a monkey discarding a jacket,
and leans forward, eyes newborn.
'Now' he says 'We will discuss
the jealousy of God.'

Iris

she rises upright, sheds
night like raven feathers
to become another,
light-engorged, turns
through sky, strong palms
the earth, pushing arcwise
against the grey gravity
into that fiery corona,
vast ring of burning palps,
sea-anemone tentacling
the oceanic clouds.

flying so, in solitary
ceremony, she opens
to the taloned sun, belly
clawed, opens to release
the mystery. yaa, life
like liver, torn, tawsed,
devoured ceaselessly.

whatever god, goddesses,
rise, ride that road beneath,
between trees barked
like snakes, whatever comes,
goes on that highway,
she heralds, guides
with rainbow gestures,
gravid, she greets
every day and births colour,
distance, calving knowledge
into the blur and cluster
of dreams, unfurls that
simple glory daily. habit husks
her beauty, lids my sight

only the birdborne orison
sometimes stops my steps,
pearls my lips in wonder
and. I, mothered, murmurless,
now only for a moment,
worship at the shining shrine
of she who rises upright
shedding night like
raven feathers.

Jack and the Radioactive Boy Scout

Jack is set to save the world, or so
he tells me. What he does with wire and paint,
with old baked bean cans opened
like clamshells, is answer more than art.
He calls them his knights, an armoury
of concepts, fierce and sharp as flame.

I don't laugh at youngsters now. I recall
the boy who built a dream with thorium
like Lego, block by block, powered
with the hands and figures of old clocks.
His generation seeped out like oil,
like smoke into the neighbourhood barbeques.
Those old timepieces ticked away again,
outside their faces. The cops called in
a hooded squad with boots and gloves
to bear away the pieces of his aspiration,
to lay them deep in the forgiving earth.

Jack says the earth does not forgive.
He sees Gaia in his dreams, dark and bright
as the revolving seas. She tells him
about revenge, about stones rising to their feet
like bears, trees sprouting pinions and claws.
When he wakes he returns to his workshop,
welds more small bright warriors.
He needs legions, battalions of spears,
before her last wind scours the sky.

Jack-in-the-Books

He showed rare tenderness, a careful touch,
and women, tired of haste and selfish fumbling,
surrendered to his arts, for he was such
an acrobat in esoteric tumbling,
his tongue so silver-quick, his hands so skilled.
A gentle man who knelt at Venus' throne,
he would not leave a mistress unfulfilled.
His spur was love, not mere testosterone.

One night, tormented by a heartless game,
he turned to rage. He did not sink to rape,
that was against his kind, but still, his shame
burned deep. Did guilt decide his future's shape –
to be entombed by tomes, by sapless shelves?
In life we find, in death we lose, ourselves.

Jerome and a Theory of Nails

Jerome is discussing his mediaeval site, where many nails
have been unearthed. Usually they rust away, he explains.
Just the sharp red sockets remain, ghosts of connection. Metal
was always precious. He bites into the tender waves

of a radicchio heart. Most societies revered metal. Malleable magic.
Makes me think about crosses. Say the crucifixion detail
was short of nails. They must have used great iron buggers.
They drove one through both feet. Chunk. Chunk.

He grates sea-salt meticulously on a cloven tomato.
Say they only used one through both wrists? Hammered it
into the vertical beam above his head. Would that still work?
He'd still be raising himself to expand his ribcase, so

he could breathe. There would still be that strain on the biceps
and intercostals–quite excruciating. I'm sure it would work
as well as open arms. And it would save wood as well as nails.
Jerome, always a keen disciple of conservation.

There is a strange blend of Casaubon and de Sade
about you, I remark. He swallows a slither of Iberico ham
and mouths *Thank you* through crescent lips. For Eliot or Marquis
or meal, I cannot say. But he dances like a defrocked angel.

Jerome and a Theory of Regression

Some people are obsessed about previous lives
Jerome remarks as he twists the corkscrew
 firmly home, but I am more interested –
 Pop! the cork surrenders – in previous deaths.

I believe you fear most the deaths that
you experienced in the past. I, for instance,
have strong memories of several ends. He pours
the blood-dark Cabernet into two Italian crystal flutes.

I can recall being skewered from behind with a spear.
The point emerged here. He indicates his left nipple.
Later I was thrown from a turret. I saw the stone
wheeling past, stark in strong sunlight. I felt my bones

shatter like Sevres on the turf. Another time I was burnt
on a brushwood pyre. I heard my blood sizzle as the flames
rose. I ask Do you think Poe had been buried alive
in a previous existence? Undoubtedly , he replies, reaching

 for a slice of olive and pumpkin-seed ciabatta. In York
I was involved in an excavation where we unearthed,
unofficially, several Georgian coffins. One corpse
had clawed fingers where she'd been scratching

at the lid. Often catalepsy sufferers were buried,
then woke up, nailed down neatly six feet deep.
Let me help you to some feta and mesclun salad;
the lime dressing is my own secret recipe.

Jerome and a Theory of Stimulation

Jerome grinds Serra Nerga beans and spoons fragrant heaps
into an elegant Waterford glass and bronze cafetiere.
My faculty secretary has had his inguinal area
waxed – , he remarks, the colloquial term is, I believe,

a Brazilian. He says it makes his manhood look longer, a trompe
l'oeil, erasing the horizontal brushstoke of the natural pubes.
I thought, but did not articulate, that it seemed a small return
for what I would imagine such an intense intimate agony.

He went to the new beauty parlour – unisex, he stressed –
to receive the epilation and mentioned that he was considering
colonic irritation, which also features on their bill of fare.
Apparently six or seven pounds of detritus can be flushed out

of the adult alimentary tract, and an infusion of coffee
is a preferred enema. I asked if he would favour Java
or a dark Tanganyikan blend, but I fear it went over his head.
Of course, according to legend, the effects of coffee

were first noticed by a goatherd, who saw his charges frolicking
after consuming berries from a certain bush, so tried it himself,
savouring the subsequent excitation. Caffeine is insidiously
addictive. A colleague of mine swallowed up to ten cups a day,

and then suddenly abstained, on the solemn dictate
of his homeopathist, substituting tisanes of camomile
and ginseng. The withdrawal symptoms were significant.
He often thrust his head and shoulders round the door

of a lecture-room, snorting like a Minotaur, bellowing
at one student while the rest of the group trembled in silence.
Attention levels certainly rose in proportion to their apprehension.
To soothe his nerves he took to sucking on an old briar pipe

bequeathed to him by his grandfather. No doubt the weed
he burned in its bowl was more modern, but it smelt as if
it were part of some ancient mummifying ritual. Jerome pours
mahogany liquid into gold-rimmed porcelain cups, so delicate

they are almost transparent. Between them he sets a matching
cream jug and a bowl brimming with demerara sugar, the colour
of aged kidskin. Probably, he muses, it's only some historical
accident that we don't smoke coffee and brew tobacco.

Judas as a General Theory

Prologue
Like – the friend you thought was your best friend but
suddenly deep kisses you, and you so not gay, and trying
not to wipe your mouth, attempting to laugh it off – there is a jolt
ahead. When it comes, you'll recognise it. You have counted
up and down to it, tock tick, tick tock, tock tick.

1.
The sky smiles down, and promises, yes, it will stay with you
always, and the sun will remain alight, stars will sing for you
every night. Yes, small birds will hatch and fly, yes, dragonflies
and treefrogs and water lilies and sea-otters and soft grey seals
snoozing against rocks. Yes, everything waiting, all possible,
until your lips are smeared and you want to wipe your mouth hard.

2.
They can warn you, paste up runes and crosses, carve
letters into skin, but you do not see, you do not bleed,
not then. It starts with a mouth unfreighted by words,
with lips bitten by silence, with sly glances, with a trickle
of pain. Remember the tree you climbed, dragging yourself
up behind your shoulders, that sudden height beneath you,
a new vision. Next day, fire across your shoulders,
as if fresh muscles had grown solely to groan, solely
to remind you that you were grounded.
Pick pock. Pick pock.

2½.
That was when the light began to creep away, clouds
blowing like feathers between your fingers, a slow
unfledging. Your aching, unwinged shoulders, the sullen
arch of ribs. Darkness seeped in like ink then,
up the wick of your body, filling your palate, till
your tongue was stiff and blubber-bloated,
till you felt fevered for some coming passion.

3.

Perhaps some lucky ones stay innocent, walk
through the gnarled wood with their garlands fresh,
with violet gaze. Perhaps some never see it coming
with its saucer eyes that ape the moon, with night
buttered on its back. Sometimes Grandma wakes,
wraps patchwork round her shoulders, chases
dust from her doorstep with the big old broom, snaps
the door tight against yowls and growls and jowls. Or
the axe falls like lightning splitting the trunk. Or angels
read the blood-spell on the door, and rattle by.

Epilogue

But not for you, sucker. Listen, the world is puckering
up like a buzzard's anus for one great wet smacker.
Take it on the chin when it comes. Your fingers
ticked down to it, a dozen to one, two hands
together, and the chime will make your eardrums
rupture. You were asking for it all along.

Jungular

A leopard leaps the space between
our bodies, its hide patchworked
gold and midnight, its chatoyant gaze

striated like Argus eyes. Its breath braises
the air. The air grows leaves, the leaves
sprout twigs and branches. The branches

unfork to trunks that spew up a rich
and running forest floor. Milling insects
spring from legs and wingtips, bright birds

uncurl from calls. Colours crowd close
and blur the distance, humming
like mosquitos. Musky lichen hennas

my fingerpads. I close my eyes to find
words and a small jewelled lizard
slips between my astonished lips.

the keep: a mirror form

the keep,
a curved stone tooth,
juts below a scumbled sweep
of oyster-grey and pearly blue.

Thunder shakes the eastern view
and wakes old lions from sleep.
In war, all truth
lies deep.

Kelpie

The head is always a horse's head, heaved huge against your own.
One risen from the sea, dark as depths that squeeze light shut.
Its neck streams against night, an arc arrowing to the rafters

of the sky. On those filaments, you can rise, abandon heavy earth,
hear flint farewells struck by metal, see sparks spit fat as stars
as journey's wake kicks backwards, a jet hurling you out into ever.

Green eyes, great head, heat against your face, hooves hammering
distance into stone, tamping it, trampling time like meadow and nothing
to fear, nothing, only ocean far ahead, the broad path moons pave,

and on the other shore, and on the other shore, sure.

Knot

This poem is not about Death,
nor about the unravelling of light.
This poem is not about God
and the persistence of revision.
This poem is not about the Earth,
its green-blue presence in the dark.
This poem is not about my body
and the way food tries to eat me.
This poem is about something
I do not wish to consider – like
confessions of impermanence,
shifts in stress, the sliced corners
of my sight.

La La Land

Come and live in La La Land
where the atmosphere is bland,
where everyone is very sweet
and all the poems are a treat.

If there's something not quite right,
please don't yell and start a fight.
because the status quo is grand,
and that's the rule in La La Land

where nothing's wrong and nothing's sick
and nothing cuts men to the quick.
If some dark inkling irks a poet
we must advise him not to show it.

Please stay in step and stay in line
and everything will soon be fine;
for we're all good and we're all free.
Let's write and publish, merrily.

And what we write is all (although
it may be judged on whom we know
and how much influence they wield).
So, sorry scribblers, shut up! Yield!

And if you wish to sidestep strife
you mustn't sully art with life.

Last Orders – The Movie

I'm ordering a Hollywood decline.
The symptoms are ideal: not being sick,
the application of a pale lip slick,
some floaty scarves, a duty to recline
against silk pillows being brave, while friends
and family troop in with gifts and flowers
and wet-eyed memories of golden hours –
stock shots of surf and seabirds when it ends.

Spare me the vulgar things, like diarrhoea,
depression, pain; they're for the hoi polloi.
A dying will seems such a good idea:
I want a starry close, so please employ
soft-focus, and cue choirs' *Ave Maria*,
then fade me out with Ludwig's *Ode to Joy*.

Laura's Feet

(with apologies to Petrarch)

I love Laura's feet
so small and so neat
still sweet in the heat

when she slips off her shoes
I smell violet cachous
the breath of her toes
like the sanctified rose
exhaled from the gloom
in the tomb
of a saint

which she ain't.

Lavender

His flesh is cartography,
a palimpsest of old engagements:
bullets, knife, grenade fragments,
powder burns on one thigh.
Sometimes he tells her, often
he starts then stops, sometimes
he is unable to begin. The things
he tells her are enough and more.
He tells her about the heat
and the cold, the waiting,
the sensitivity of it all.

She gave him the essence
in small iodine-glass bottles.
He uses it to treat the blisters
on his feet. At first he worried
that his men would laugh, but now
they all carry lavender. The thought
makes her smile, the fragrance
of elderly English ladies carried
into the little hells of the world,
over permafrost and desert.

In Grasse the purple acres raise
a scent so thick, you wouldn't be surprised
if it knocked larks out of the sky.
The oil is pressed and collected,
concentrated yet so gentle
it can be applied neat to the skin.
When he leaves she says, Take care.
She dabs her pillow with lavender
each night. They say it aids sleep.

Lepidoptera

He paints butterflies and moths
resting tremulously on flowers
so delicate you are afraid to breathe
lest a warm waft lifts them
away from the paper

his beloved brushes, chisel tipped
or sucked to a chinese point
arranged in a dark bronze jar
like a bunch of smooth stems
streamlined ikebana

tubes and cakes of paint
laid in careful spectra
piled paper like scented sheets
in a linen press
aching to be touched

he mixes alizarin, black,
ochre and white
precise as a pharmacist
dilutes, inspects, dilutes
then floods a new white sheet

when it dries and shrinks
it will be ready
not quite white, washed
with the whisper grey
fainter than a gnat's shadow

on this he draws the outline
of wings, a peacock eye,
antennae fine as shrews' hair
the flower comes later
born from the butterfly
a reflection of its wings

both hover on the page
suddenly alive
see the butterfly
scenting the flower
you know it is a trick
but it is still magic

in the corner is a still life
five crushed red lager cans
brash as whore's kisses
bills, books, magazines,
a mouldy bread baton
conducting a trio
of orphaned socks

you wonder if it is
installation art

perhaps if you stirred it
gently with a mahlstick
you might unearth the chrysalis
of his crumpled rainbow soul

Lies

Perhaps it's true, as Twain implies,
statistics are the greatest lies
but point for point and size for size,
I think they tie for major prize
with poets' modest little 'i's.

Like this

Like this: a grey-eyed girl
dreaming of darkness
under an afternoon sun.
I'll give you the colours:
French blue and tangerine,
long greens and earths.
You can supply the sound-effects:
a small drone through grass-blades,
crows creaking in the oak,
and something pushing up
beneath the pauses between.

Afterwards you might think of them
as portents, the noises
and the colours – I forgot
those redbreast apples
ready to drop but waiting –
for now, they are simply
weights in the balance,
parts of that hot heavy day.

Look back at that girl, couched
on green, but say nothing.
She is poised between past
and future. Your words would nail
her to the present. In this garden,
silences crouch in a shadow
like toads growing jewels.

Listening to the Dog

My dog is teaching me to die. He explains that humans
think too much, confuse thinking with wisdom. Each moment,
he says, is a world that time cannot touch. I had forgotten.

His course begins with learning how to gather up flesh,
with feeling the brain open like a flower, the taking in of breath
hard, until it burns the lungs. Lungs will not be needed.

I will seize his shaggy throat and he will pull me through the elements
as the dolphin drew Arion up through the eye she had made
in the skin of the sea. Eyes will not be needed. Vision will become

being. Beyond there will be grass greener than the smell of rain
and no sadness. I believe him. We carry our feeding bowls out
into the garden and fill them with sun. Bowls will not be needed.

The Little Princess

Constantia lives in interesting times.
The tumbrils grumble past. New hopes, old rage,
dark gossip, whispered names fill, page by page,
the catalogue of real and rumoured crimes.
She dwells above politic pantomimes,
as if her future plays out on some stage
where heroines escape a bloody age,
sublime, aloof, like poets' paradigms.

She knows Papa prepares her proper match
and trusts all nastiness will pass her by.
Her life is still a perfumed perfect dream.
for she is lovely, lively, rich – a catch.
Her maid pins young Constantia's ringlets high,
red-ribbons her slim throat *à la Victime*.

Little Town

Bethlehem is blockaded,
the priests are sent away.
Tanks are standing in the streets
so no one dares to pray.
O Holy Holy Holy,
the gods of Chaos say.

Livia's Eagle

When great Augustus croaked, Rome yearned to see
great signs. His widow would not leave desire
to chance, I found. My captain hissed at me,
"We'll see an eagle leave the Emperor's pyre,
winged like his soul." "Thus Vestals prophesy?"
I asked. "Thus Livia commands," he grinned,
"before the fire, you'll slip a cage in, sly,
a trap will open: bang! Our bird's upwind."

I did my part, but then the damned spring stuck.
I climbed to set it free. The crowd guffawed.
Her set, white face. My lousy soldier's luck –
those bastards laughing, when they should be awed.
But, Jove, what sod would let an eagle burn
although he earned a roasting in return?

Longing

In the morning, love, I yearned for you
with exultations of the oak-throned thrush.
I sensed your breath in every tiny rush
of wind that stirred green fragrances of dew
and moved sweet flower-drifts and scattered seed.
You always lingered just beyond my sight,
a promise at the golden edge of light.
My hands reached out. My heart was huge with need.

At last I wearied of desire, and grew too tired
to hope. The business of the world, its grind
and grief, devoured my time. Grey sirens mired
my course and I was lost, but now I find
your presence at my side, where you have always been,
to crown me with the stars that I had never seen.

Lorenzo to his Lady

When Isabella found her lover's head
she buried it inside a basil pot;
convenient while he was freshly dead,
but when his brains were roundly rotting, what
excuse did Isabella give for smells
arising from the soil, what careful curb
could she put on decay? Corruption tells
and surely basil's not so strong a herb.
If, dear, you potted part of me, which part
would your sweet fancy choose to keep enshrined:
my lights, my liver, buttocks, hands or heart?
I know that you don't love me for my mind.
Ah, love, though clerics claim the flesh is vile,
fond thoughts of rigor mortis make you smile.

Lucifer on the news

You tell me the earth is bleeding –
so what? The old bitch is in heat again,
forging a wake of blood-spots
as she whines at the sky.
Tell me what you think she summons
from the darkness, what lurks outside
the yard, sniffing, cock twitching with must?
Oh, the angels of light would be at
the latch, flinging the gate wide.
They worship fertility with every quill-quiver,
but they can't fuck – there's the juice.
They'd hover over the whelping
like cramp-bellied buzzards. Sex
thrills them, the mad abundance of sperm,
seed and spawn lavish as Solomon's wealth.
They swoon in the vicarious heat
of passion, melt in mirrored comes,
eyes raised and narrowed to lasers.

Spread your dark wings, lads, drive off
the dogs, ride shot-gun to prevent
that curse of belly. I could have snipped
the cord long ago, ended the threat,
but the governor claims it's unnatural,
that all possibilities must be allowed.
He won't open the gate, but if it were
to swing ajar, with a breeze, a waft
of pinions, a nudge of sandal-sole –
well, that's already accounted for
in the long-range plan. It's his job
to dream, and our duty to act.
Dip the buckets in Lethe, fill flasks

189

with citronella (save the garlic
for my gazpacho). Shrill the great sirens
and launch the squadrons to deep swarm
again. Bugle me, boys, and remember:
brightness hides the enemy.

Lying Together

No doubt I seem serene and well content
as side by side, futoned, silk-wrapped, we lie.
You think you lie more skilfully than I.
I've smelt Eve on your skin, her sickly scent

that sticks like oozing sap from rough-planed pine.
Of course I don't blurt out the lies I know.
The grapevine's tendrils softly grasp and grow.
Susanne her flatmate's an old friend of mine.

We picked the pair of you to bloody bits
as we sipped Veuve Clicquot and shared her bed.
I loathe you, prick. I love Susanne instead.
We've both concluded men are total shits.

Your new love's shagging Susanne's brother, Lou:
so here we lie, we two, while Eve screws you.

Manifesto

If you can read this, please step back. It's clear
you're standing far too near the page, for I,
I'll introduce myself anon, am here
to fence your questions about What and Why.
Behold an author of the Modern Age.
Take time to marvel at my bold designs.
So what if fogies pick their bogies, rage
and fume about my fucks and abstruse lines?

What if my verse makes little sense and lacks
all logic, form and rhyme? I bow towards
the avant garde; let other sorry hacks
supply the style. My forte is raw words.

I steep myself in darkness, drugs and drink:
A poet feels, you fools. Let others think.

Marsyas

My song was ripped and flayed
when they cried 'strip it bare'.
Behold its keening bones;
the muscles bleed elsewhere.

Martha in the Morning

Sweetheart, help me through this day.
If cousin Jean should start to say
'Ah, well, he's in a better place,'
I swear I'll slap her in the face.
And help me to suppress my rage
if someone mentions 'ripe old age'
as if that means there's less to bear.
I can't decide which hat to wear.
Look, here's the one you always joke
reminds you of Queen Mary's toque.
I like this fancy feathered one –
but half the stitching's come undone.
Dear Edward, help me do my best
to lay you peacefully to rest.

Megaera in the Cocktail Hour

She is standing with the dark-eyed man
in the corner. He is twitchy with his glass,
casting glances at the wall where the clock
escaped. It is because, his teeth remarked,
he has to be elsewhere, locking the gate
against defenders. She has been through
several sieges, has eaten ripe, unnamed flesh
and sucked on roast rat-tails.
She reaches down with tended talons,
tweaks the rule of stockings
which she wears on her shinbones
as a statement of entente.

Icebergs clink in crystal,
liners cruise proud and unprepared
across the carpet. Passengers wave
from the shore, their journey in the air.
She is growing feathers as he squirms.
She preens, pecks, crows 'Darling.'
He is nestward bound, destined
to feed her green and gold fledglings. The rush
of wings bears him out into the carpark
and pins him to leather. He has no chance
to semaphore. He misses Mayday.

Meg Merrythought the Milkmaid

Meg flirts her skirts as she sells Guernsey milk.
She smiles, beguiles and winks – her comely way
more flattering than any lady's silk –
and hints she'd love to roll you in the hay.

See how she puckers for a kiss, her tongue
luscious as a strolling snail, limbs lithe
as otters in the millstream, flesh as young
and supple as sprung wheat before the scythe.

You know you are her special boy, her prize,
her punterkin, her apple dumps, her chuck.
If you were skint, she'd give you one for luck,
not for your pennies but your big blue eyes.

What do you think sweet Meg is thinking as she fucks?
She's wishing you the pox, the plague, the bloody flux.

Memento Mori

A white spider-husk on a torn web.
Rattle of winter branches. Feathers and fur
bristling in an owl pellet. Broken birdsong.
Sunshine auburn through dry beech leaves.
Twilight. Moonrise. The dint of a fly
on a pond's meniscus. Sheets of newsprint
ghosting across the carpark. Dark spectrums
shifting on an oily road. Pain in the lungs.
Closed eyelids. Open fingers. Raindrops.
A distant dog voicing the night.

Mermaiden

She sits on a pearled imperial rock,
scaly buttocks snug against the shells.
Limpets lickle at her fingers, pedicure

her tail-tips. She sighs, tastes the salt
on her lips, thinks of sailors, a mariner
with tousled chest and blue-irised Irish eyes,

sweet matelot, a sea-dog she will leash
with the Hokusai whorls of her hair,
burnished like sunbeams on wave-curls.

She combs her locks with honeyed words,
blows kisses at the lusty gulls, hears their shrieks
climax on a hump of landed orca.

Her heart is brine, harder than Lot's wife,
baked and caked by long years on the flats
of water. Her eyes are liquid, like her song.

Beware of her beauty, as cruel as the ocean,
as eternal as the wash of waves, the wane
of shore. She is in her element, you are mere

mammal, juicy and ungilled. A subtle mind is nothing
more than tissue. She will lace it on the swell
like marbled fat on meat. She will dissolve you

into her queendom. You will spill guts, groin
and begetting into a sudden maelstrom
of sharp reflected stars.

Motorbike

I saw in a Hollywood film
that you can outrun
a tidal wave
on a motorbike.
I thought of Steve McQueen
who never made the great escape
but still revved and bucked
like a true hero.
I dream of easy riding
the wide open road,
an aery highway
that spans huge country.

No need to fear nature
when we can mount a metal steed
and fill the night with noise.
Behind us, the water crumbles
buildings, streets, bridges.
Beneath us the throb
of the engine;
ahead as much freedom
as we can swallow.

Mrs Buggins Considers The Big One

I worry sometimes how it will be after
the tunnel, you know, which sounds like
the Tube, without the tourists, but lots
of neon and rushing noise. Yes, I shall go
towards the Light. Try and stop me.
I'll be hurtling, hurdling any unwary cherubim
that get in my way. But no, to be serious,
when I get there, if there is a There,
and if I get there, what will it be like?

I worry, you see, that they'll be right
and I'll be wrong. So many say they know:
gurus, mystics, priests, all those smug
snug believers, even the Jehovah's Witnesses,
will they be there, shaking their haloed heads,
trying not to smirk, not to say I told you so,
as I'm directed to the Basement? And will God
be there? I nearly said He but I've never believed
in a God with Sex – but It sounds odd – then God
is odd, at least to a mere mortal like me.

What can Cosmic emotions be? Doesn't Love
grown so vast start to get echoey and cold?
But I like to think God will be there
and speak without words, take me gently
without hands, laugh at me for my questions
but answer all with endless patience.
I hope there will be trumpets too.

M Theory

In the Eleventh dimension
there is a knot
that prevented strings unravelling.
The Eleventh dimension
was embraced by Super Gravity.
The Eleventh dimension is
incredibly narrow yet extends to infinity
and holds a Membrane
in which universes sail and swerve
into fierce collisions.

The Eleventh dimension is the stuff
that fashions dreams
of the wholly Grail,
yearnings for the Theory
of Absolutely Everything.
We are pimples
vibrating
on the membrane
of a planet
circling a small star
in a universe
that rides storms
through the Membrane
of the Eleventh Dimension.

It may be as simple as that.

Mudlarks

They step down the slippery stone to the dark river flats.
In the evening sun, the Thames stinks of centuries,
filling their nostrils with Saxon wood and Roman iron. The rubbish

churning in the sludge quickens like silver through his brain.
He adjusts the earphones and tunes into waveband Hopeful.
He can hear coins clanking in lost barges, clinking bottles wired

with Victorian ginger and rotgut spirit. While he scavenges, she leans
against greened bricks, foraging a head stuffed with velvet, conspiracy
and steel striking fire in cluttered paths. Gulls swirl down

foul-beaked – the same harsh brood that Marlowe marked
and Johnson cursed with a forehead wrapped in vinegar
and Latin phrases. She feels the marble bulge of St. Paul's

as close as her childhood, the old nursery rhyme fresh
every hour. Every hour, the waters roll by, tawdry grey
and sluggish, cleaving the city, unmindful of the wide sea waiting.

Multi-tracking

Professor Dwight is bright, all smiles today;
I sharpen up my ears like Mr Spock's.
He likes smiles. Grin, you fool! the voices say.
Don't mention mother-ships or talking clocks.

Professor Dwight enquires about my dreams.
Last night I rode on fiery doves with God.
Don't tell him that, you nut! I hear the screams.
"I don't dream much," I lie. I smile and nod.

Professor Dwight is writing in his book.
I try to read the letters upside down.
Don't act like that, the voices say *don't look.
The shrink could lock you up for good, you clown!*

He asks about my medication. "Well,
quite good." I nod. *More crap!* the voices yell.

The Mushroom Effect

Isn't it strange, my husband said, *that heliotrope*
is purple, when it sounds so golden. Even so, I am drawn
to the dusky shades. He asked the stationer to find
some heliotrope ink – eventually the man mixed it up himself,
from blue and crimson and a tincture of black.
That night I had been ill – I didn't like to say it
but I blamed in on the dish of wild mushrooms
gathered in the fields. He's so easily distracted.
The dandelions the French call *pissenlit*,
he calls ghosts of sun in moonlight, though
I was taught the botanical name. Father rolled

the syllables off his tongue,*Taraxacum offinicale*
and split the stem to show the seeping juice like milk.
Pissabeds, rustics call them, for their diuretic grace.
Their roots can be roasted and ground and brewed
like coffee. And the fragile clock, the head, a mass
of seeds poised on quivering filaments, so delicately
attached, like the full round of the mind, like sanity.
One breath and it scatters on the wind.

But the cook sanctioned the mushrooms
with a dainty sauce of orange and cream
so tempting that I swallowed the fungal slivers
almost before I realised they were on my tongue.
And then my belly woke me in the night, bubbling
like a kettle. I used the chamberpot, then wrapped
the quilt around me, found paper and pen and wrote.
My ink was plain navy blue. My nib rode on my words
like a yawl on an Atlantic swell.

I wrote of a wood where trees were branched flesh
over pale hoods of fly agaric, *Amanita muscaria*,
and of a woman with eyes instead of nipples.
My nightmare terrified them all that evening.
I thought perhaps I should send my husband out again
with the old oak trug to gather his ambiguous harvest.
Art, I realise, requires risks, consumption
of the secret sunless things. Now I often dream
of dandelion seeds drifting over water, swept
back to the shore like small winged spirits,
pale and mute, never finding sanctuary.

My father and The Sopranos

My father would have liked *The Sopranos*.
Not that he was a great family man,
but he would have understood the scripts.

He knew you had to raise your fist
occasionally to ward off wrongs
and keep things in order. He would

never acknowledge past violence –
It was a told story, passing into legend,
not real any more. A story about Jupiter,

Jovian, jovial, something to be chuckled about,
a fable of what a man must do
in the face of fate. So it was woven

into the tapestry, the colours fading
on every viewing. My father appreciated
dark humour. He worked at night. He did

the shifts and liked the freedom.
He had another life behind the scenes.
He would have sympathised with Tony,

shared a drink or two, a joke.

My Life with a Latin Professor

Lorenzo has been taken by aliens again.
They caught him four nights ago in the car park
of The Conjuror's Half-Crown, took him up into the starry
starry night, as he puts it. The mothership was retro,
tricked out with silver plastic and plump crimson velvet
like a '50s cinema foyer. They freshen the air
with a lemon-grass scent. I smell it on
his jacket, one tone above the cigarette smoke.
Nicotine is a habit that hit the greys hard.

Last month I was carried off by a band
of raiding seraphim. The smell of incense
and burnt plumage lingered between my thighs
for days. I hummed Holy Holy Holy as I vacuumed
mats and rearranged our dust with feathers.
Strange how he and I remain such tempting prey
to skyfolk but perhaps the conjunction

of pheromones that first brought us together calls
upwards like a signal beacon. And abductions,
these enforced absences, are in one way welcome
lacunae in the mundane act of togetherness. Who knows
where Lorenzo will be next week, or how far up
I will fly. I do not envy our friends' uninterrupted
coupling, their drab separations by appointment.

Tomorrow I may be radared by an eagle
seeking a swan. Today I scramble five eggs with milk,
not forgetting a dash of mustard, and spoon
the pale mimosa into two willow pattern bowls.
With wholemeal toast and strong coffee, that will see us
through till lunch. We step out under the open sky
like eyelets waiting to be hooked. Our history
will be as much vertical as horizontal. Our hearts
are always thudding like wings.

Naming of Parties

How should I introduce you now ? Um erm,
you are all man, so it would seem too coy
to introduce you as my current *boy-*
friend, such a mutton-dressed-as-lambkin term.
Significant (ugh) *other* makes me squirm
and *lover* is too bold, describes too well
what we do lustily in bed, and, hell,
a *partner* smacks more of some legal firm.
I can't endure an antique *paramour*
or *beau* in tow, and *steady* is a hex.
My other half would make me laugh for sure
like *mate*. This nomenclature's so complex.
Sweetheart, perhaps we should stop having sex –
far simpler to announce you as my *Ex*.

Namu's Nath

One night the blood-red gem fell from her nose.
She let it lie for memory's sharp sake,
and soon the skin, long-pierced, began to close
and heal, and time began to blur each ache.
Perhaps love's vintage was a little soured
but she received a letter in his hand;
apologies and lies her heart devoured
and in return forgave as it had planned.

Ah, if the ruby stone were not in place
when they next met, and those dark eyes should miss
his loving gift's rich glint upon her face,
his questions might delay their greeting kiss.
She pushed the slender shaft through knitted flesh:
so ever women's pain and pleasure mesh.

The Night Emile's Mistress Turned Into a Cat

She raised one arm above her head.
That was the start of it, a smooth
stretch of muscle, a lengthening of bone.
She was resting on exhausted sheets,
fingertips touching the wooden bedhead.
He heard the scrape of nails.

He lay beside her, drowsy with coming,
and drifted into dreams, her rump spooned
in his belly, firm against his soft sex.
He awoke to a narrow vacancy,
her furrow parched and empty.
The mattress ached.

She left a ghost of warmth
and three golden hairs on the pillow,
glowing like marmalade. Sometimes
he hears a serenade in the lane
beneath his window.

Queans sing when they disengage,
briefly, bitterly, then they lick, clean,
clean, forget.

nighthouse

when I broke into the nighthouse
you'd already cracked the lock
standing sky-eyed in the hallway
picking apples from the clock

grandpa slumbered in the attic
breathing like a chickadee
as I watched your wicked fingers
lifting heirlooms off the tree

but you turned to me like nothing
angels cradled on your brow
and I saw your leopard grinning
knew you'd stolen wings somehow

when your finger touched your lipfold
I was thinking of your tongue
though I knew your sails were setting
once the summer dawn was sung

you're a robber and a raider
dusty dry dock buccaneer
velvet coat and pirate pockets
crammed with someone else's gear

sack the magic and the silver
thieve the music and the score
I hid one red shivered treasure
that you'll seek for evermore

No Fear

"Go in fear of abstractions" - *Ezra Pound*

A fucking big dog, it lurks in my front garden,
nosing the re-cycling box. The hair on its muzzle
is stained and frazzled like a smoker's beard.
But when I go out to post refuse in the bin,
it looks at me with kind eyes, brown as caramel,

soft as fudge. It's a dog. How can I dislike it? Large
and innocent it lumbers beside me up the path
and through my front door. It smells as damp and dirty
as good sex. I can't resist it. My house is its kingdom,
my couch is its day-bed. I attend it with can-opener,

canine treats and ignorance of changes to my Axminster.
Once the beast is installed, I am transformed.
It is like love, but we don't need to mention that.
I feed him, he licks my hand. Few metaphors
are so simple, so satisfying. Call it serendipity.

Noli Me Tangere

At first he wore a labourer's hat, with shovel brim, but he threw it
over the wall. His hands were hard and bleeding,
but she wet them with her tears and wiped them
with her hair until he was tangled in her skull.
At first she flattened to the earth serpent-bellied, but he raised

her spine like a ladder. Angels climbed and fell like herring
in a shoal, like a swarm of gnats globed over a lake.
At first the sky was black, but the sun ripened like a fruit
and burst into the sea. When all was burning, burning,
but nothing was destroyed, when breath was stilled,

he stretched out one hand to pierce the horizon. He drew out
a leafsome branch, and after it, the tree, and after it, the roots
that held the orchard, and underneath, the gold, the ground,
the golden crown and thousand pinions.

No place like home

where you were cradled, rocked, where your soles first rolled on grass, on
stones,
where you first looked up and saw a dome of stars like God's hand
cupped above you,
black, cold, huge beyond towers, beyond mountainous trees, where you
learned words,
where words became stories, and stories swam in music, and secrets
lurked like sharks.
where you grew up against a wall like an espalier, and your trained limbs
reached out
further year by year until your fingers touched a rift and you left yet the
bricks came
with you in a suitcase with books and clothes and something lightening
like love
so you could carry it all, floors and windows and the roof-tiles wet with
rain and the way
the wind howls and whines and prowls like the lost dog you call night after
night
never knowing it is asleep in your bed with a snore like ancient thunder.

No Shit

After seven beers and a chicken biryani
Jack was suffering from constipation
which was not at all the usual effect.
The expected hot flood remained
in his mind, while his bowels strained.

After a while, he grew tired of it
and ripped off some paper to wipe
his arse, but as he made the first pass,
he felt a sudden loosening that liquefied
his knees and sent him slant across

cold tiles. There was a heaviness,
an issue in his cupped hand. He drew
the crumpled tissue in front of him and saw
a gleaming curvature. It was larger than
a hen's egg and warm. After a moment's

wonderment, he pulled off more paper
to swaddle it then tucked it into his breast
pocket. He picked his way carefully through
the restaurant, magpie monochrome against
red walls, avoiding waiters, wined lovers,

and the plundered sweet trolley,
feeling his heart beating against twill.

Not Much

I didn't ask you for much – only to stay with me and to stay strong
and beautiful. You were fleet and fierce, your fur flowed in currents
I could not feel. You rolled in the surf then dried yourself
on the sand. You rubbed against me, stiff with salt, and laughed.

I didn't ask you for much – only that days like that should remain,
that they would stretch out into years. You never walked to heel,
but quartered the ground before me. You were my pathfinder,
my defender. Fear dissolved in the shaggy turn of your throat.

I didn't ask you for much – only to remain with me, for I'd learned
how much I needed you. Your hind claws began to drag. One day
I found your paws bloody. You'd walked on through the pain. Failure
spread up your legs. *It grows faster in young dogs* the vets said.

I didn't ask you for much – only to deny the inevitable, only to fight
an enemy that had already downed you. You didn't ask me for much,
only leave to retreat when the battle grew too long and harsh,
and a time to lay your head in my lap and gaze goodbye.

dedicated to Cresset,
the beautiful German Shepherd I lost to CDRM (canine form of MS).

217

Number 30

On the road to sunny Boscombe,
On the jolly yellow bus,
We're all standing nicely,
Loath to make a fuss.

Churk churk goes the engine,
Jeeeeeez protest the gears.
Around that hairy corner
We were nearly on our rears.

Thrown this way and the other
As the driver revs the wheel,
Listen to the wind whump past
As stressed tyres squawk and squeal.

Tut tut says the business man,
Ooooh sweats the harassed mum.
The pale priest starts to count his beads
And thinks of Kingdom Come.

Then up pipes the dear old lady
Lavender lace and cross,
"Who the hell d'you think you are,
Stirling Fucking Moss?"

Nursery Rhyme

Into my childhood attic,
while I and Polly played.
there came 3 jolly grenadiers
in red with gleaming braid.
They look so charismatic,
my naughty Nurse confessed.

Hooray for 3 brave grenadiers!
They searched the big pine chest
in search of golden loot.
Inside were only books and toys
and a little silver flute.
Polly and I grew quite afraid,
listening to the noise they made,
and Nurse burst into tears.

Now we start another verse
with 3 grenadiers, not so jolly.
who drank an oath
and cursed a curse,
and then things went
from bad to worse.
They rode a cockhorse,
abused my dolly
and finally they rifled Nurse.

Remember, children,
parrot Polly:
Life is short
 and war is folly.

Nuttin' to do with Marvell

If I had trees enough, and time,
your pillage, squirrel, were no crime,
and we could could feast on endless nuts –
but now I've come to hate your guts.
Because my garden is so small,
you're leaving me no nuts at all.
I asked politely, 'Please depart'.
and you responded with a fart.

So I will get my little gat
and shoot you, fuzzy-ended rat.
I warned you once, you had your chance.
This is no furry-tale romance.

The Obligatory Autumn Poem

Leaves browning, crimsoning, yellowing
papering to veins, small maps of hell.
In these fadings for Fall's deep fallowing,
ten thousand farewells as they fell.

Fruit crowning, colouring, mellowing,
plumpening wild crops with Ceres' spell.
In these seedings for Winter's harrowing,
sweet kernel of the new year's shell.

Ode to a Mature Male

O, Sweety Plumpkin, did you know
that, as men age, some parts still grow?
Their ears get bigger and their nose,
But, alas, not that–though look at those!

Ode to Ozzie

Poor Ozzie's only 52
See what rock and drugs can do.
By the time he's 53,
he may look as wrecked as me!

The One Hears an Occasional Bomb

The One hears a bomb, and shakes his head.
He watches like a tired tele-journalist
documenting a pride of lions. They sleep, rise, kill, eat,

sleep. He does not interfere. That is not his business.
He watches. Sometimes a colour, an image, catches him
unawares. The refraction in the holy lens swells

into a droplet of light. A jackal moves on the outskirts
of his pride. He grew fond of it and named it Death.
Sometimes he feeds it. His pride feeds itself.

The One spins worlds on a great wheel
like lumps of clay. He rolls them into place.
This is his business, the Making. He stands,

and presses his palms to the hollow of his back.
He aches. He watches and aches, but
he does not interfere. One day a serpent

will rise up from the pearly lake that gleams
like an eye at the core of the universe,
rise up with throats and question him. Only when

he hears the questions will he understand.
Until then he will turn and fire worlds
and position them in the dance of force.

Once they are placed he does not intervene.
He watches pride yield to pride. His arched back
aches on a long bass line and the orbits sing

in piercing graded trebles. Their notes weigh
heavy as a crown on his brow. Through the music
he hears the bomb but does not interfere.

One of Seven Seraphim

As soon as I emerged, I was drawn
up by the cord, which he braceletted
around one wrist, and I spiralled upwards
on a purple worm, tickled by pepper clouds.
I felt his flight, the rise and thrum
of pinions spatulate upon the aery strata.
Upworld was bright and throbbing, or so
it seemed against the vessels of my eyes;
Downworld I felt on my heels and buttocks
as cold draughts jostling my flesh,
but both muted, veiled by movement,
as he spread horizon like a salve.
Above, a strange vibrant choiring;
beneath, a deep dark resonance.
The arc of the spectrum he commanded
jade, rim of indigo shimmering like silk,
turquoise blue, shadowed, azure,
shot with gold, rich as peacock plumes.
He spoke through the small kingdom
of his stillness, hovering like a dragonfly,
the dazzle of his wings, palpable warmth
on my face and belly. And so
I learned to speak. Flying came later.

One Reason to Love

Subject: The discovery of connections.

Argument: from observation
Someone throws you a line, and you gulp it
like a rising trout, the spinning feathers engulfed, then
turn down into the boiling waters, and spit out the hook.
The feathers fly again, as pheasants, peacocks, larks,
claiming the air as their element, inflating the sky with song.

Digression: the purely subjective
I hear the intricacies of their melodies, those rills,
those skeins of notes, as if they match the map
of my nerves, synapse by synapse, as if they were made
for me, a robe embroidered with my name and nature,
needlepoints marking the flow of *chi*, Maori lines
inscribing flesh, skin as mythology, a tattoo of blood-beats.

Corollary: subjective presented as objective
The connections which bind the water to the air,
the sea to the mountain, a mind to eternity,
sensed in the thrill that moves across a night calm
after its black was ripped open by electricity,
red forests seen in embers, a far planet striated
like grapefruit segments, the brain washed with lemon
after fainting, euphoria after a migraine.

Coda: the possibility of resolution
Heraldic creatures which faced away from each other,
inlets and outflows, heads and tails, tips and toes,
now fold together like a sheet of paper
halved, like words bleeding ink as they touch,
like the click of insect genitalia, like a Chinese box
solved, opened, and another puzzle inside.

On Philip Larkin

with apologies to Edward Lear

How pleasant to know Mr Larkin
who has written slim volumes of stuff,
who partook of Earl Grey and parkin
and declined to be seen in the buff.

His manners were British and donnish
(one won't wear one's heart on one's sleeve),
traits that a Yank might admonish,
asking, 'What did this mother believe?'

Some delved in laundry and letters
for a cad with promiscuous needs
but sex clamps us all in its fetters,
and he left us his words, not his deeds.

It's rumoured that Larkin was clever,
so perhaps, in the end, it is best,
to let his words speak out forever,
while the poet enjoys his long rest.

They say he loathed blacks, wogs, and Zion,
when bigoted push came to shove,
but his verse shows what humans rely on:
the almost-ascendence of Love.

Opening a Jar of Dead Sea Mud

The smell of mud and brine. I'm six, awash
with grey and beached by winter scenery,
pinched by the Peckham girl who calls me posh,
and boys who pull live crabs apart to see
me cry. And I am lost in that grim place
again, coat buttoned up as tight as grief.
Sea scours my nostrils, strict winds sand my face,
the clouds pile steel on steel with no relief.

Sent there to convalesce – my turnkeys, Sisters
of Rome, stone-faced as Colosseum arches –
I served a month in Stalag Kent, nursed blisters
in beetle shoes on two-by-two mute marches.
I close the jar, but nose and throat retain
an after-tang, the salt of swallowed pain.

Opening the Box

Dawn breaks, a shock of red upon the moon;
the growling in my guts begins again.
I know what apparition comes at noon,
a feathered fire-eyed phantom, shrieking pain
and guilt, for I devised the foulest crime.
My theft betrayed my kind. I stooped to raise
a lesser breed, and so for deathless time
the mountain chains me, tortured in a maze

of thoughts. The fierce head hunched above my chest,
the slimy gobbets gulped, my flesh a feast,
and worse, this furnace in my mind and breast:
the knowledge of the evil I released.
I gave men what they craved to fight the dark;
now burn in conflagrations from that spark.

The Other Woman

I met your wife in town today. Calf-eyed,
she spilled the spoils of silkworms' guts, rich cloth
designed to grace her figure at your side
and, as we chatted over latte froth,
I pictured her prim mouth reamed wide with shock
if I told tales about your wicked tongue,
the times I taste her juices on your cock,
and how we scale sin's ladder rung by rung.

I see my revelation makes you start.
You like our secrets, her dumb bunny trust.
The intrigue and the danger speed your heart
and stir your lust. They power your first thrust.
Enjoy me now. My interest's soon spent –
I find love more exciting when it's lent.

Painting in the Garden

I used to spend so long on foliage, dot
by dot, I'd Seuratize the leaves. You changed
all that. Thank heaven for a Master knowing what
was what, and how affairs can be arranged
with flair. You painted by a defter plan:
a fan-shaped brush to lay curved colour down.
Your fingers brushed my wrist. Your sleight of hand
laid subtle drifts of green and gold and brown.

The eye believes that these quick strokes are leaves
and conjures up the living rounded trees.
Ah, what small signs the ready heart receives
to conjure up its world of fantasies.
Illusion is a snare that sly art weaves –
you caught me naked, one of many Eves.

Painting the Ceiling

All things evolve to ending, slow or fast;
this is the way of life, that nought endures.
I know all fades and one day cannot last,
but this dawn I awoke and sky assures
me that forever lives. The sun
fellows me, mellows me; I breathe his gold,
the hollow vault above, a blessing won.
I will not feel impermanence and cold.

I am axis, atlas, ball and socket joint.
All light flies to my eyes. My quick thoughts touch
the cynosure, define the focal point.
I radiate horizons. Lines rush
to me, tier on tier and rank on rank.
If I am not, the universe is blank.

Party Piece

You were telling me about someone who couldn't find
a colander, so drained conchiglie with a tea-strainer,
a spoonful at a time. I wasn't sure if it was a joke, or about you
or your sister, who died from breast-cancer two years ago.
I visited her in hospital on Boxing Day. She lay there scraped

and grey, sandwiched between two holidays. She got
the nurse to twine some tinsel in her hair, and tried
to drink the Cava that I'd brought. We talked about nothing
for hours, then watched TV, her hand in mine. You said
you weren't fond of pasta – they serve it up too much

these days – and I mentioned I cook noodles for my dog
and toss them up with cat-food. She won't eat dogmeal.
You told me about the Birman who sits on the keys
whenever you open your laptop, giving you an ice-blue glare.
Then Nikki started to sing one of her Hebridean songs,

her voice husky with Dewars, a song about love and time
and betrayal, so we all grew quiet to listen. After a while,
I noticed you were crying, and so was I, but then Big Ben
chimed fruitily from its tower, and after toasts and kisses
and firework volleys, our tears were lost in the opening year.

Passing

The fact that I am naked makes me
shiver. The others who pass by, with
blurred faces, do not notice that

they are treading on my shed clothes
and skin. Air is winter on the crimson
of my flesh, my nerves combed

like flayed wires ready to be twisted
to the current. I am caterpillar small,
yet my frosted breath fills the room .

All who pass are suctioning my lungs.
I cannot breathe. I have to run
outside, where the night is opened,

and though I left them bending over you
like vivisectors, you walk beside me,
long stride curtailed to mine, bare neck

arched and one untubed arm pointing
outwards to the endless dust of stars.

Pavements

The sun brings out small lives.

I step carefully
across a trek of ants,
over a bumbling humbug beetle
and a grounded fly.
I scoop up an apple-juice caterpillar,
loop it into the sanctuary of a shrub.

I see others walk on regardless;
some tread on spiders.

How do the gods walk?

Penelope Agonistes

Where I live, there is a room
and by the wall, a wooden loom.
Every day, I spider-spin
to let the rainbow patterns in.

I let the rainbow patterns in
and lubricate my throat with gin,
and weave my deep poetic stuff
sitting starkly in the buff.

Sitting starkly in the buff
till nosy neighbours shout : Enough!
then I close the window blinds
and curse them for their narrow minds.

I curse them for their narrow minds
but a weaver quickly finds
solace in another glass –
so Philistines can kiss my ass.

Phonophilia

O for a Muse of aphrodisian fire
to paean Chloe on the telephone!
What siren-song could match her sultry tone
which charms the ear and stirs the loins' desire?
Her breath weaves fantasies across the wire;
she wakens members, hears men moan and groan
as they massage their own erotic zone,
and burn like twigs in lust's consuming pyre.

Her venal voice enthralls the rapt receiver,
as hot as Monroe toasting JFK
and huskier than Dietrich's dark cachet.
Alas, sweet Nymph, you are a sound deceiver.
A fag-end dangles from your chip-greased lips
and big grey knickers panoply your hips.

The Pismire Oration

Kreck, kreck, the Plumeys have been down pick pick
again. The valley-balls, the lupes, the liplap danglers
are all mussled and distrayed. Who was scooting
on the oakmost roam, and did not give the larum
to beware us? We could all have been mordered
in our buds, culled in curls and couchings.

O my simlings, gather round in heedance.
First we must brush and bellish, make bloomheads
clean and sparkish, then we can cusp and susp
and I will tale you tellings of long days ago,
stores of queens and trells and hellent warfor.

Ho, hard there, fattyfiller, with your seggy bodments,
do not munge upon these leaves. Peel off
and mandicate elsewhere. This pliant plot,
this green clingdom, this is our heapsake,
our hill-land, our gem set in a sylvan lea.

Rejuice, my simlings, simsters. We'll browse avids
on the fallage, surp meet mead nectar soon.
All life is ground and gladly – part from Plumeys.
May Magog smart the flockers from the highs.

Playing God

I met with God along the Pilgrim's way.
We shared a six-pack on the trampled verge,
and when He asked me if I'd like to play
a game of travel-chess, I felt the urge
to question Him, though I was rather shy
and doubtful of the Lordly etiquette.
As He set out the pieces, I asked "Why?"
God echoed "Why you suffer? I forget."
"Are we just pawns?" I asked, and moved one out.
He chose a knight to leap the humble rank,
and said "Don't ask Me what that's all about;
the bishops say it's Satan you must thank."
I carped "The Primal Cause is You, alone!"
God said "I'd love to chat, but that's My phone."

A Poem by the Green-Eyed Monster

O my God, these poets. How they nature on.
Their pieces are stuffed as full of leaves
as a nursery, as full of birds as a rookery.
Do they write on trees, say, inscribe their words
on sheets of hammered bark? Perhaps they pull
reeds from the river, pound them into pulp
to make their rustic paper. Do they really live
day-to-day with their heads up squirrels' arses,
with nuts and catkins like a veil before their eyes?

Why is it so hard for me to believe that they draw
water from that old cold well, and squeeze dough
between their inky fingers? I picture them
in their armchairs, just like me,
watching the latest coloured crap
the TV companies provide. Just as modern
and unnatural, just as full of e-numbers,
however hard I read the labels, just as
dislocated from the primal re-creation.

But somewhere they buy the Wordsworth glasses,
the Tennyson titfer, and the greenest ink
that monks can muster, and off into cloisters
of forest and streams and mountains merrily
they go, journal in hand, quill-gilled.

And I am here, dammit, with a huge red dog
snoring like pre-Genesis, squashing my toes
and there goes the Green Man stalking past
disdainfully as I tip-tappity at the keys
and hear the rustle of a crisp packet
lodged beneath my unpoetic bum.

The Poet to His Lady

I sent my servant with this letter, Love:
you left him standing in the city's rainbow flow,
abandoned in the common street below
your casement, where your chambers jut above
close merchants, tradesmen, nobles, whores together –
the evening stream. He braved the jostling pack;
returned with long curls dripping down his back,
his features like an emblem of the weather.

You left him waiting in the way, small rain
a-piss on him, his new cap in his hand.
He turned without a word. I understand
my sonnetelles were spurned, my verse in vain.

O Mistress, whom the moon and sun adore,
that was my final page. I'll send no more.

The Poet's Dam

Mothering, murthering, mild as a doe,
sharp as a hawk, shifting, stark-mad,
Ireland hurt you into poetry, man.

Green-shawled, her face weathered
by the firelight, she sucked at a pipe
with the sound of damp peat hissing

on the flames, rocked you, oaken-throned,
while outside, lost gods hunched and humped,
like great hulks looming through a sea-fog.

She spoke you great men and little folk,
the endless dance across the grassy river,
battles and bloodshed, faeries, fatal gold

and dragon-guerdon, heroes and hunted,
hauntings, hatred slanting through the years.
Morphing her masks of goddess, crone

and maiden, she spelled you to her hearth,
webbed your lad's heart as only a mother can,
careful and cruel by turn. You flinched

from her blow, and received a caress.
She suckled you in old lore, sustained you
with long songs, starred your gaze,

locked the legends through your hair,
laced your feet into seven-league boots
so you could stride beyond blue distance

if you wished; but whist! Her fingers pluck
at your coat-tails, so you linger
by her ingle, waiting for her broth,

the blessing of her breath.

The Poet's Fall

I will arise now and walk beside the lake
where drifts of leaves persuade me heapily
that Autumn is at hand, holding a palette primed
for my painterly pen. Here are abundant birds,
geese, ducks, etcetera, to wing in a melancholy skein
across my page. This is the very stuff
of poetry, dead leaves and distant feathers.
Let us not think too much of flesh, of sex.

Lovers are safest dead, to be remembered,
for twilight birds to name in the complaining wind.
I may recall the dint of a warm head in my lap
but no lolling tongue or grosser body portions
will soil my watercolour world. I dip my nib
in pristine ink. Ah, such mistiness, such pastel grace!

The Poet's Wife

There's a bee in the bedroom curtains,
vibrating against the glass. It will escape soon,
to unearth sky. Yesterday you reminded me
that all the worker bees are shes.
Listen to the plump throb of her body.
They stack the wax hexagons neatly
through the hive – such strength and economy
in that sixfold architecture – and pack
the cells with females – a few drones
the only males, mere generation-fodder.

I know your Muse is female:
I have smelt the vanilla of her breath
as she speaks into your ribs,
and twists her fingers in your heartbeat.
I see her hair tangled breaklessly
in the fabric of your eyes. She teaches you
the heaviness of teardrops,
the melt of bowels, the aching pull
of womb on vertebrae.

You call her Anima. Her wings of blood
fade and flux with the tide,
strong as light, timeless as sorrow.
Mistress of subtle mysteries,
she lifts your face to the moon,
softens your sight, cradles
the earth in your cranium,
and she lies between us, humming,
as you cast your gaze around.

police dog

he's a police constable
but he has a plain-clothes voice
a friendly Northern burr
warm as a fresh chip-butty
he moved from Oldham
to the countryside of Cumbria
he likes to walk the fells

he doesn't see
the organised crime
but the domestics
often upset him
he says you work eight hours
then you have to cut off

he's been working
with the drugs squad
he tells me about a sniffer dog

who noses in car crevices,
cupboards, cubbies
the coverts of a home
suddenly gets excited
the handler perks up
leans forward importantly
scenting drugs

the spaniel
eyes aglow,
tail windmilling,
proud as a pea-dog,
unearths a bar of chocolate
he's always finding chocolate

I laugh
the policeman grins
he says they're dreading Easter

A Pong Song

Sepia breadth of a Celtic bog
with centuries of mattressed peat,
moss fruiting on a goblin's log,
the distant plash of joggers' feet,
Triassic ferns, quick slick of frog,
dim memories of earth in heat,
deep autumn hedginess of hog,
the musty pleats of piddled sheet,
compote of grass, thick-tendrilled fog,
two shakes of salt, one glob of meat:
That's the smell of big wet dog.

Prose or Poetry?: A Philosophical Investigation

I think
therefore I am.

I think I can write poetry
therefore this is a poem.

I think this is a poem
therefore I am a poet.

I think I am a poet
therefore I am,

I think.

Pumpkin Pie

He'd sworn that she was not his type, too thin
with, at the most, three-quarters of a mind
and, Geez, that laugh – a gerbil drowned in gin!
He'd stressed again that he abhorred that kind
of wet-lipped tart with slap fit for a clown,
all tawdry flesh and flash, a laughing stock,
hems hoist like flags and necklines plunging down:
sure signs of too much mileage on the clock.

His wife soon read the tale in Visa's sums,
his statements contradicted, line by line;
how odd a modern fairytale becomes
when fantasy and fact and lies combine.

That ugly sister was a myth – instead
he'd had a ball in Cinderella's bed.

A Q-mail from the Inner Ring

In the Intergalactic cafe, they've banned aftershave
following a series of explosions involving violently
incompatible pheromones. They still serve mocha tea,
pickled lignum, the stew of small blue livers. I listen
for the squall of your jets, but you never come.
The shuttlers arrive for the a la carte, smoke
their pinchong pipes and sing. They tell me
you were seen on the rim of Gaias, stringing
lovers like pearls on a wire.
                                   Not that I care now
my brows are bound in jessamyde and silk,
not that I care now I rule three green
and gold planets, not that I care
about you, not that you broke
a single one of my hearts.

Quartering

Sir, I was taught to write
by a former master when I was young.
He had enlightened views they say
but he died childless and his estate
fell into other hands.
I was not needed so I took the road.
I could have fallen into crime
but by God's grace I found my calling.

When I am about my business
sometimes I hear the tinkle
of fine china and silver
from the open windows round the square.
It reminds me of my days in service.

The hardest thing I find is not the hanging
nor the burning nor the gutting
but the first cut that takes
the manhood. I cast it into the fire
without delay. I keep them on the rope
longer than most and have been censured for it
but my purse is no fatter however much
a wretch suffers. I take pride in neatness.

Often the press and sound of the crowd
hit me like a fist. I smell the stink of rut.
I wash my hands and arms and return
to my family, leaving the work behind.
Once I told my Confessor
that thoughts trouble me at night.
By Our Lady, he said,crossing himself,
Without the rule of Law
We would be as beasts.
You are God's instrument, man.

Now I must excuse myself
for the fawn cow is big-bellied
and close to her unburdening.
Last time I had to remain all night
beside her. She bore a white calf
as dawn rose over the beechwood.
My eldest daughter called it Puss.

Raptors

("E'en then would be some stooping" –
Robert Browning, 'My Last Duchess')

Today we step out for his sport and pleasure
across the wide estate, trout-streamed and wooded.
The Duke calls for his pets, his feathered treasure,
and cadge-boys bring the birds, gold-belled and hooded.
My lord extends his leathered arm, his eyes
as bright as claw-set gems that stud his fist.
He scans a perch and picks the sleekest prize,
a full-summed peregrine to grace his wrist.
She cuts the morning wind, a grey-fletched arrow
dispatched to strike the prey. She stoops, kills cleanly,
then mantles jealous wings to claim the sparrow.
A merlin stirs and snites. He eyes it keenly.
"Hush, sweetheart, hush," he whispers, maiden-mild,
and strokes it like rich silk, a coin, a child.

Reflected Fly

When the light hit her cheek a certain way,
reflecting some small darkness, that tear looked like a fly,
one of those loud black furry bastards settled

on old meat. Your hand in the same light looked darker
fleshier, rarer than it had, lonelier, leaner.
Your could feel it tingle with a strange charge

after the numbness. It only hurts the first time.
Then the anger settles like a bluebottle,
fat and heavy, spewing juices as its nature,

feeding on what it has prepared, tenderised,
because the fly spews itself on to its food.
After the first time, you learn the trick.

Your mouth doesn't go dry. Your juices flow
naturally. Every sound that food makes is only
a variation on its consonants and vowels –

merely another plea to be consumed.
Meat had better learn that silence suits it best.
And so you move from maggothood to mastery

of the air. Your wings unfurled and stiffened so soon
and that first giddiness, that tiny lurch,
is soon forgotten in the noise of navigation.

Rembrandt's Angel

Mine's a large port and lemon, the angel said, stashing
his wings behind the bench. Drink always loosens
his tongue and stories rose like moths
to dazzle against my ears. *Last night I dined
with Rembrandt,* he said, *The old boy told me
that if he went back, he'd be a poet, not a painter.
I told him there aren't enough words for all
the earths he used, terra sienna, seal, russet, walnut,
brown ochre, burnt amber shading into umber.*

*Those flat winter afternoons melting
into evening when darkness treacles
into huddled corners. Light your lamps
and candles but the night shoulders in
with bruised eyes. His son died at twenty-
three, consumed by the world, and afterwards
he celebrated, year by year, all the small
deaths in a face, lined loss and laughter,
busy as village wakes, and always,
beneath the flesh, a festival of bones.*

*Why did he want to be a poet? Simple, words
cost so little, a goose-quill, ink and paper
would supply all he needed. Instead
he beggared himself for pigments,
lapis, orpiment, vermilion and jade,
hues from the huge open-arsed world,
precious and poisonous. He ground
and mixed them as an alchemist,
gilded canvasses with colour, but*

257

the round gold was slow rolling in.
The lean wolf was at the door, howling
with the bastard bailiffs. Remember times
when he laid golden fruit thick on his easel
but ached for a loaf of bread and the holes
in his stockings big as biscuits and potato-cakes.

So he decided, yes, next time he'd use words
not paints, because the application
became too much, the long struggle
with brushes as if he were wrestling
a wild hog to its knees for the bristles,
or the sables turning on him with sharp
snug fangs and driving him to bed hungry
and dissatisfied, eyes puffy and belly
a-grumble like small coal in a scuttle.

The angel paused. *Buy me another port*
and I'll tell you about Milton wanting
to paint, he said. I obliged but mentioned
his usual tipple resembled a sick man's piss.
He raised the glass to the light till
it winked, and sighed, *Ah, Pasteur, now....*

Remembering the grapes

He sucks his finger thoughtfully,
running his tongue over fresh ridges
where briars snagged his flesh.
A strong, handsome lad, arms and shoulders
shaped by working the Umbrian soil,
now he thinks of the vineyards, and curses
the day he took up the sword and the standard.
Not that it's any disgrace to uphold
the Pax Romana, but sometimes he misses
the smell of rich damp soil in this parched land,
feels weary of an alien place full of dark religions
fermenting like grain under the sun, Zealots
and priests all gabbling beardily,
eyes bulging like barrel-bungs.

Tomorrow he will offer a pair of pure white doves
to Jupiter and ask to be posted back
to his green hills. Who can feel at home
in a land where the sky grows dark in the eye
of a bright afternoon? He never wanted
the bloody execution detail; daily splinters
were bad enough, but the thorns crowned his discontent.
Leave them to it, he thinks, and dreams
a burst of red grapes in his mouth,
first draught of the new vintage.

Riddle

When I was a swan my neck
was a proud curve, yes;
I braved the wind and water
and launched beauty,
like a longship on the flood.

When I was a dog, I ate warm grass
from the bellies of my prey,
felt packed muscles under pelt.
I ogled the moon and howled.
Her face gave me my clue.

When I was a bat, I hung
through light and flew the straits
of night. Hunched in your hand
I blink blearily at you,
my grounded body curved.

When I was a snake
I waited in the grass
until I found the right angle
of trajectory. Look,
I begin to turn into leather.

When these creatures are combined
you will find my whole in mind.

The Rime of the Ancient Mountaineer

Beware, he stoppeth one of three and said,
"I am an Ancient Mountaineer and snow
has bleached my eyes. Cruel frost has gnawed my head.
I seem an abseil-minded loon but O
I have a tale to tell. I conquered heights,
my faithful bergschrund at my side, and scaled
great stones of sky. We shared rapt days and nights
in realms where couloirs of the rainbow paled.

We watched loud flocks of pemmican, and saw
the dainty serac leap from spur to spur.
We climbed to Kingdom Cwm through ice and thaw,
but now the mounting bliss becomes a blur:

I raised my crampon, – ah, my heart was rock, –
Alas, 'twas I who shot the alpenstock."

bergschrund: the gap or crevasse between the glacier proper and the upper snows of a face.
couloir: an open gully.
crampons: steel spiked frames which attach to boots giving a more secure footing on ice and firm snow slopes.
cwm (pronounced COOM): a deep rounded hollow at the head or side of a valley, formed by glacial action.
serac: a wall, pinnacle or tower of unstable and dangerous ice.

the rising flight

we were listening
to an old album
like amber it holds
an ageless girl

singing an ancient air
in the Gaelic
a Celtic knot
plaited of love and pain

her voice like fingers
touching wet strings
draw out the chords
of my well tuned heart

the melody swoops like a gull
above sharp rocks
always in the rising flight
the danger of a fall

you refill my glass
with rich red wine
touch my cheek
with your fingertips

say nothing
play the song again
always in the rising flight
the danger of a fall.

Rite

I felt the rough hemp
that bound my wrists
and with the halting
of my hands
my ears grew filaments
into the fire-flecked air
the darkness hovered over
me like eager crows.

I was silent
I know enough
to hoard my words.
the earth wheeled
towards morning
as I waited.

It came to me then
on old furred feet
and whispered
into my nostrils
fierce heat
a din of dragons
and the weird
of the great worms
who feed on the roots
of the world-tree.

After that,
the hanging
was merely
a formality.

Roi de Verre

They filled a glass Byzantine cup, blood red
as noble swordsman's shame. My taster tried
the wine. I watched the wholeness of his head
fall back, the gulp, the gasp. I think he died.
Before I smashed the venomed vessel down,
I saw the gleam of sacred gems, the sly
encircling eyes, glazed light around my crown.
Now all is dark. Both day and night I writhe
through dreams. Astrologers consult their charts.
I feel black fractures branching through the bone
from where they bored a blowhole to my brain.
One day my flesh will shatter into shards
and no one, nothing, will repair my throne.
A crazed glass holds the fragments of my pain

*Charles VI of France was also known as Charles the Mad. In his madness, he cut
down several of his own men. He sometimes put iron rods in his clothing as he was
convinced he was made of glass and could break. A trepanation (operation to bore a
hole through the skull) provided only temporary relief.*

Rouge et Noir

The Queen of Hearts is bored; she stretches, yawns
and winks at black-eyed Jack, then swiftly stakes
a crown on one turn of the cards. It dawns
on her, of course, speed kills, but still she aches
for thrills. Her life is flat, her days unruffled.
She fancies other games and chooses stud,
but she forgets the pack should be well shuffled
and Jack cons every deal – it's in his blood
to mark each play. She calls. Her hand is decked
in diamonds, her face flushed with success,
but he holds all the aces. 'I suspect
you cheat' she cries. Well, look for knights in chess.
Let's call a spade a spade, and Jack a knave
who plays at love and loves to misbehave.

Sally's Song

Sally sits on the arse of the day,
her slammerkin ribbons all astray,
blue in her hair, red round her throat,
smelling the cullies as high as a goat.

The London road brought Sally down
into the grey and gaggling town,
away from the fields and the delving cold,

into the capital, twelve years old.
Smile now, Sally, don't you frown,
though the streets aren't paved with gold.

Your Ma is dead, your Pa's a sot.
Feel in your stocking for what you've got.
Your petticoats hide such tight young meat

so sell it while it's hot and sweet.
Another tickle, and God willing,
another trout, another shilling.

Let's go down to Tyburn Hill
to see the robbers dangling still.
The raw gin makes your stomach lurch.

Lace your gown to make cocks swell
and paint your lips as red as Hell.
In satin slippers, trip by the church.

Blue in her hair, red round her throat,
smelling the cullies high as a goat,
her slammerkin ribbons all astray.
Sally sits on the arse of the day.

*slammerkin: type of dress with a tight bodice and a skirt open at the front to show an
under-skirt.*
cullies: a prostitute's clients. Literally gulls or dupes.
Tyburn: site of public executions in London.

Salt

The mer-folk, they who drew us down, for aye
have lingered in the chambers of the sea
till God's own sunlight makes them flinch and cry
and seek the human salt of you and me.
They round your eyes with coral gems and pearls
and xylophone your ears with magic shells.
You dally-dangle with bright mermaids' curls
and feast on bounty, fresh from briny swells.

But lads, remember you are sons of earth
and darkling depths a strange unhallowed space.
Think on the blessed land that gave you birth,
the holy breeze, a mother's kiss upon your face.

Down here, my shipmates, far beneath the waves,
I smell the churchyard grass in Neptune's caves.

the same difference

some women wear the britches
some men wash the dishes
some men are quite saintly
some women are witches
some men are bastards
some women are bitches

Some women are freewheelers
some men find quiet niches
some men are true as turtles
some women scratch their itches
some men are bastards
some women are bitches

but when they hike the hitches
and share their worldly riches
bitches don't pick bastards
and bastards don't choose bitches

The Sandalwood Horse

There are in world, many kinds of sandalwood, like white
and black. The substance is compact and hard, and gorgeous.
Sweet smell stays forever. It will avoid all types insect,
so keep happiness and luck and safe. This horse is carved
as kind of handicraft or piece. The method of carving is very fine.
It is best work of art and worth to collect and appreciate.
In the meantime it is decorating your home. We know
you may like the likeness of this horse which is 3 inches
rearing lifelike. Thank you for looking at our good.
We hope to ship you horse or other sandalwood thing.

Santa Cruz

By Mary's Grace, my king appointed me
to launch a fleet against a bastard crown.
Though we were ill prepared to bridge the sea,
and my long weary sickness weighed me down,
my king demanded speed for his grand mission.
I lay near death, scarce capable of speech,
while he vowed – hot with fierce ambition
for holy war, the sermon He would preach –
that soon God's ships must strike with fire and sword.
I could not plead delays, nor dare a lie.
Half-blind, perhaps, but still my sovereign lord,
he bent perforce to catch my faint reply:
Your Majesty, I answer from my heart,
there is no man so ready to depart.

Sasha's Mug

Sasha had a special mug with a fault
in the firing, which sang when it was filled.
It cheered us all up, that high fluting note
from the shiny caramel china.
I remember sitting with her, earnestly discussing
the Wife of Bath,or Donne's Devotions,
while Welsh Mary's bed thumped against the wall
next door because her boyfriend was visiting.
'Not much to look at, but his family is loaded'
she shrugged.
　　　　　　Those regular bangs and the sound
of Sasha's mug, occasional calls down the corridor
for carbon paper or the cheese-thief's name,
a glug of kettle-fill from the communal kitchen.
Life was so simple then. The flaws in the glaze
resolved into song. There were always blackbirds
outside the window, never crows.

Scrappy Mike

Stand in the corner, Scrappy Mike,
you're such a rowdy little tyke.
You can't go hitting who you like.

Gee whiz, he criticised my bike
and told me I could take a hike.
I call it a pre-emptive strike.

senryu

everything turns
on the lathe
of God's laughter.

Sex Kitten

She loves dating older men.
It's not their experience
or their intelligent conversation,
not just the fact they don't understand
going Dutch, and the rumpy-plumpy
of their wallets,
or the way they pull back chairs
and open doors.

It's mainly for that moment
when they unveil Tintin and Snowy
and she gets to take a good long look
and say,
Have you heard of Grecian 2000?

as if for the very first time.

Shackleton's Dogs

This is the nature of the hero:
After the dogs have burst their hearts
dragging hard cargo
across the burning snow,
they were dragged,
whining, yelping,
one by one
shot, skinned
and eaten.
The heroic soul
has little room for compassion;
it is lumbered too full
with ambition, certainty
and the unconquered distance.
Perhaps heroes,
being bred of gods,
demonstrate to us
the icy set of divinity,
the very nature of the beast.

Shahrazad's Earrings

The citrines in her tender lobes
were peach juice petrified – bright globes
that snared my gaze with orange fire.
My heart was ambered in desire.

Shedding a Little Light on Light

'To explain its full nature,' the ferret says,
'would require a more brilliant tongue

than mine; but I can provide a few pointers,
if someone will stow my mice away for me.
I stuffed them with chestnuts and chives,
so I don't want to lose them. Rodents
have a habit of disappearing round here.
Take that as a starter – while light is, mice

do not vanish mysteriously if you keep
your eyes on them. Light comes
from the sun or the moon, or the fire
which flowers in trees when the sky forks.
Light strikes our eyes and shows us what
is what and where is what. That is useful.
Now, you may ask me: how did light
get into the sun – but does it matter?

I feel it was the work of some great ferret,
a hero of our race; but I have no proof.
Light is good and beautiful, and I approve.'
He removes his spectacles, and checks
his turnip watch. Tucking a furry roulade
snugly under each arm, he toddles out
into the tooting street, humming an air
from *L'Arlesienne*, greeting old friends.

The Shell Game

The teeming sky descends upon the beach
with claws and butcher beaks. From birth
prepared to fight for life within hard reach,
the hatchling turtles clamber to the surf.

Draw back: the shrieks will fade – a rain
of seeds, a fertile storm. Can I find worth
in worlds of waste? Ignore the nerves, the pain,
this billioned dance of death across the earth?

If I could stand, stand not too far, nor near,
perhaps I might perceive each fragile shell
a sun, each drop of blood, a healing tear.
I try to see like God. Perhaps all's well

for some can look, and think, sans irony,
on wheeling rims of stars: All this for me.

Sholey

Sholey brings the summer in a shiny old tin bucket
every year. He walks head high across the mountains
carrying the flowers. In the brim of his wide hat
nestle songbird eggs in pastel clutches. Sholey
holds the rainbow in one iris, in the other is a pool
of music for the crickets and the treefrogs, for
all the strange small creatures. Sholey is the father
and the mother, gardener and guardian.
Sholey waits and watches, all the world his ward.
When the season withers and blue sky is widowed,
Sholey is a sexton, who stands bare head bowed
in shadow, till he feels earth pulling at her moorings,
then he rises,and polishes his pail, brushes clean
his felt fedora, pulls on his walking far boots and strides out
to the periwinkle foothills, lungs full of tomorrow,
hullooing lanky blessings to the bright beloved stars.

Shopping as an Act of Faith

Light buoys her up. Dawn parts
the blinds and burns into her ribs.
She dresses slowly, binds
silk around her torso, listens
to the radio, aware of incoming waves
through her flesh and her wet organs,
deflected by her skeleton into a shimmer
on each high note. A soprano
sings; garden thrushes hunt for snails.
Somewhere in the sky, there is a room
without hardness, without vibration.

Outside the air is green. Deep draughts
of it are heavy, bread in her lungs. People
push too close. Fragile as a wishbone,
she keeps close to the railings. Her radio still plays,
open-throated at the window; Carmen's red flowers
trailing farewell down the street. The music
drops away from her ears, petal by petal. Clouds
shutter the sun. The light begins to leak away.

Shopping for Fruit

*('Every morn and every night
Some are born to sweet delight.' - William Blake)*

Marjani walks to the market with her sister,
the houseboy three respectful steps behind.
Her lowered eyes travel on her feet
which sweep like brush-twigs, swirling
the dust. Her sandals sweep away the thoughts
that crowd her path, sweet thorn, the span
of gnat-wings, a mountain's shadow, all
inside her head, circled by a tussah scarf.

Her fingertips linger on a bolt of indigo cloth, plump
as a thrush's breast. It sings to her of arches,
deep-shadowed gardens, marble fountains
behind elaborate gates. Then it slides beneath
her grasp. She curves her palm on a melon,
fat and orange, presses its navel to test
the ripeness, lifts the small heavy bellies
of figs, green weights sweat-sticky on her flesh.

Beyond a white wall, prayer rises to heaven
in a hundred coloured strands. *The sky is the holiest sight,*
she thinks. *Surely God's eyes are blue.* Her sister
cradles plantains. They both wait for the needful child.
This evening, with well-washed hands, she will prepare
a meal for the unknown husband who comes near
only at night. Marriage is strange and sharp as smells
that curl from the Somali neighbour's kitchen. Spices stirred
by gold-bangled black hands, pink when they open.

When her husband is away and his mother snores,
Marjani steals outside and unveils her shoulders
to the stars. Now she holds bright air in her fingers,
tastes the sun on her tongue. Once she had words,
but they flew away on a blue silk bird, beyond the hills
inside the sky. Now she smiles, silent as a new-laid egg.

The Silkie

Mhaire works in the kitchen,
her feet in her own greasy dust
which she daily scours away.
There are chicken feathers in her hair,
fishbones between her toes.
Her hands are red and rough
as ovenbrick. Her eyes are slate.

Words mean nothing to her now;
she is shawled in the song
of the waves. Sea-winds whisper
in the kettle, steam over the soup.
Leeks smell of kelp, carrots snap
like lobster-claws, turnips turn
into turtleshells. Pale starfish
lurk in cloven tomatoes.
In the convolutions of cauliflowers,
in their white coral cerebellums,
she finds him:

his salty, shining eyes, his midnight mouth,
his bones galleon-ribs, arched over
a heart loud as the surf-surge.
He calls to her from the evening waters,
from the moon's kingdom.
He will wash away kitchen,
lave her fingers soft, turn maid
into princess.

Each day ebbs a little more.
At night, on a sheet of sand,
her muscles liquefy.
Silver fishes shoal her bowels.
The ocean shakes its creamy mane,
rises on strong green knees
and carries her away.

Sirius

I was an old dun dog who followed Christ
through the wilderness. He put his palm
on my head, and I saw all things as they were,
bright with water, ringing with light.
I fed on locust-fruit, St John's bread,

and at the end of forty days, I lay down
to die. He rested beside me. I licked
his brow and heard ocean calling
from the shell of his ear. The warm waves
took me. I am the new dun dog

who swims in the beginning sea
where all things are God's thoughts,
silver as tunney, lithe as seals.
I am the size of the sun, laughing
as only a brown dog can laugh.

Sky in the Pie

Two sure cuts open the crust
and release a rush of dark thrushes
with golden beaks, heralding an arc of stars
borne on a rainbow. The spectrum flexes
like muscle, then settles in a single depth
of colour, blue as the powdered lapis
on a manuscript page in a rich book
of hours, blue as a dunnock's egg, blue
as distance. Take your spoon before
it elopes with the knife, and taste.

The clouds melt on your tongue
and sweeten your throat. You can chant
this day across the meadows, and call the lost flocks
home. The sheep and the chestnut cows. The dappled deer
and wild black horses. The wolves and small quick foxes.
All the lost beasts of your kingdom.
Call them home.

sleepwalking

the awakening feels less real now
than the drifting away
she curls her toes to hold
the warm night beneath the duvet
feels the wrench
as she arises
her reflection in the bedroom mirror
not Aphrodite
more Artemis emerging
chaste and chastened
from the lake of Moon
bone weary of the business

a sense of withdrawal
of pretence
of assigning significance by habit
to what no longer matters
she thinks of it like
the shift from one phase to another
the lunar faces
expressions that melt
blurred voices
movement of hands
sleepwalking
walking with sleep
a gentle preparation
for the long dark to come

ahead the slow sweep of hours
and the pain
and beyond
so far beyond
the other kingdom waits

Small Sister Mary

Small Sister Mary-Magdalene of God,
sleep golden in the corner of wide eyes,
descends where many sandalled soles have trod,
the morning garden scents a sweet surprise,
and sweeps a regimen of stony stairs;
her instrument a faithful old twig brush.
Her head is filled with psalms and plain sung prayers
and thoughts of crumbs to feed her speckled thrush.
She dreams a lady on a skyclad seat
while early light, through ancient tinted panes,
casts jewels upon her dust-bedevilled feet
with ruby, emerald, and sapphire stains.
An amber spider abseils down her nose
and fledgling imps find lodgment on her toes.

Snakehead

Me and AJ Taylor
in his Daddy's old white pickup
chasing the high hot dream
across the ragged range
we used our cocks like weapons
the triggers pumped more slowly
from one soursmelling motel
to another asshole room
across the dusty miles
the nights ambled in laconic
swayhipped like the Duke

searching for the southlands
sensing sirens on our tails
we stole a silver mustang
parked open by an outhouse
and filled it with the stink
of tacos, Camels and cheap beer
in the glovebox a faded roadmap
a baby's rattle and five photos
of a woman sucking hogs

last night by a crooked churchsign
AJ found a starving skeethound
fed it cheeseburgers and Pepsi
scritched its ears and called it Angel
lying in the backseat
on his painted leather jacket
it scratched and burped and farted
then slept like distant thunder
as we rode the the desert road
scrunching potatochips and peanuts
waiting for deadeye Dawn
that old hick Sheriff
to nail the desperado Moon

AJ lit another Camel
found Jim Reeves on the airwaves
and I was kinda drowsing
when the highway
reared up like a snakehead
and spat us into town

A Snapshot of the Ancestors

They stand on a shingle beach, brows furrowed
by the weight of the sky. The city is over the horizon,
a train's length away. Here the sea scent swells

pale chests and small waves shiver their strangely
bare toes. I know that at the bottom of their lungs
London air lingers, smoke-grey and full of voices

but gulls are calling, rowdy sirens, and they wear
holiday like a costume. They feast on skate and chips,
and candyfloss, feed pennies to the brash arcade,

ride painted horses and circle in spoked planes till their guts
heave. Punch cudgels Judy while pierhead bands dispense
Strauss and Sousa. Their fun is as fixed as the sun.

Snickers

I have seen the Eternal Footman
hold my coat and snicker;
he recognises off-the-peg
and I tipped him half a nicker.

I have seen the Eternal Barman
arch his brows and snicker
then semaphore his cronies
that I cannot hold my liquor.

I have seen the eternal Houseman
bend his ear and snicker;
grace notes for my hardboiled lungs
and my syncopated ticker.

I have seen the Eternal Frontman
raise his mike and snicker
nailing me with quirky quips
like the ghost of Alan Whicker.

The Snot Fairy

I am a little bag of bones, humming
like old meat furred by bluebottles.
My eyes are black, my face is brindle,
but briefly I have wrapped myself

in dragonfly livery to perch
upon your shoulder. Would you tend
a wounded toad? Would you nurse
a needy spider, or caress a frog

with no princely promise? Will you
love me small and foul, tuck me
into your tender pocket? Pucker up,
and kiss me. I am the poison pips

hiding in apple pulp. I am the gristle
others spit away. I am litter, loathsome,
the laidly worm. I am ungainly, ugly,
loveless. Embrace me, buss me.

I carry no coins, no riches. I offer nothing
but the world's wideness, telescoped
into your chest. All I furnish is a flame
to light your chamber's grate forever.

A song for Lucy

Lucy bold and Lucy shy
Lucy laughing at the sky
Lucy small and Lucy neat
Lucy playing in the street
Lucy low and Lucy high
Lucy learning how to fly

Lucy warm and Lucy cold
Lucy dreaming rings of gold
Lucy false and Lucy true
Lucy knowing what girls do
Lucy priced and Lucy sold
Lucy young but feeling old

Lucy dark and Lucy bright
Lucy needing needle-bite
Lucy raw and Lucy scraped
Lucy beaten stripped and raped
Lucy short and Lucy sweet
Lucy redmorphed into meat

Lucy black and Lucy white
Lucy dances every night

A Sort of Ode to the Poem Lady

(or You Don't Have To Be a Hypochondriac, But It Helps)

Hush, they are carrying in the Poem Lady again.
She is too weak to walk herself; she comes swooning
from a room thick with the scent of sinister blooms:
hellebores, opium poppies, lilac, pallid orchids. They wrested
the belladonna from her frail fingers, although she wept.
Her dark eyes are still watery, her nerves as delicate
as a spider's network which leaves stickiness
on your fingertips if you are unwise enough to touch.
Once I tried to bring her a bouquet of peasant flowers:
stiff-stalked Piss-a-Bed, Ragged Robin and corncockle
but they turned me away with curled lips and curses.

A linen handkerchief, redolent with lavender, veils
her temples. One lily hand droops towards a pen.
A rumour ripples round the room that she will write
today – it buzzes fretfully like an exhausted bee.
She grasps the pen – the courtiers hold their breath
terrified they may waft away her strength and inspiration
but she dispels their fears. Her ivory soul shuttles
across the sheet, weaving a lattice of fragrant words:
amaranth, muscatel, damascene, vermillion, amber.

She drapes into Pre-Raphaelite attitudes as Poetry
continues. She writes of her weakness, of her womb
which is connected to the moon by silver strands,
and her sacred suffering self, her sensitivity,
her swollen heart which bleats like a sacrificial lamb.
Her tear-haunted eyes sweep the walled garden
for the Vision Suitable, for trembling leaves
and picturesque petals. She acknowledges
a thrush's distant rapture, rain patterning
her casement, the purple periphery of sunset.

From a world she is too fragile to consume,
she retreats into consumptive dreams, floating off
to seek death like Elaine on a tapestried barge.
Taken by the current, she sings of suicide and pain.
O Poem Lady, may we be forgiven if we hymn life
instead of celebrating the sickroom. O, help us
to wallow in unease and depression and shadows
as we should. For ever and ever, lest Poetry die.

Spaced

Carpenter rode the starstorms round the outer rim
of Ryga, traded blue-rockers and wreckers
and the real estate of dreams. He hard-hustled

with the skin tribes who ply, Altair to Actureus,
and mojammed all the dives that stud the systems,
sawing mean riffs on the Les Steele cithern

he'd salvaged from an ExFed skimmer, drifting
like a black gardenia petal on the dead Allurian sea.
Carpenter was a fly guy, eyeballs like a price-gun,

who knew the current value of every artefact in play.
He'd find you any offway thing you wanted,
sell you things you'd never heard of, from golden

cryoid beetles to the song-stones of Elphore.
Carpenter was a hero, the highwayman
of light-paths, a hunter and a warrior, one name

every race respected, one word everyone could trust.
Last time I heard from Carpenter, an old c-mail
off the delta, he'd shacked up with a snake-girl

and they're raising green-skinned children in a forest
of sweet gourds. Like he said, if Death don't get you,
some other bastard clips your wings. As for me,

I'm headed heartward to join the Jennan legions, bucking
for the angels in a war that spans six sun-charts, battling
for the prizes and the causes and the reasons,
fighting for the feelings that Carpenter forgot.

Spanish Fleas

He is wearing flip-flops again, strumming
the strings of the old guitar he brought
in a flea market outside Córdoba –
I said *Why don't you buy fleas instead, and start
a circus?* He laughed. Everything slides off him.
He starts to sing about dark eyes and romance.
Not my dark eyes, I trust – my eyes
are more aquiline than columbine.
His sinister fingers pattern the chords, his grip
flexing and releasing. Melody is a wordless lie,
I think, and his bare toes are grubby.

I grill peppers and aubergine, grate
white cheese, drizzle green and purple leaves
with oil from a squint-glass bottle,
while he plays the Andalucian songs,
cante jondo. Siempre, siempre he croons,
mi corazón, amor – all lies, consumed by time
like fresh leaves, like light swallowed by a cavern.
¡Hermoso! he gasped, when he saw the black
and mahogany figures on the walls.
He bought postcards of the ancient hunt. Stallions
and aurochs floating on stone, without horizons.

Our dark eyes meet above the music.
Dinner I say and he flip-flops to the table.
The guitar lies full-bellied on the couch
like a sleeping woman. I feel fleas moving
across my skin as he eats my food,
and smiles. *Corazón, amor, siempre,*
those parasitic words. The itch of flesh.

The Sparrow

I dreamed of Beowulf and dragon-lore.
bright treasure gleaming underneath the hill,
brave kings who drank from brazen horns and swore
great oaths, berserkers crazed to hack and kill,
a lurk of monsters in their murky den,
gold rings, rich torcs, and magic swords unsheathed;
all thrilled my eager childish heart, but then
I found out what these warriors believed,
that life was like a sparrow in a storm
swift-winging through a banquet-hall, from rain
and dark, a fleeting passage, bright and warm,
then through the doors to angry night again.
I grieved then for that lost beleaguered bird,
and now, for truths unsought, and best unheard.

sphinx/sphincter

once I think (or more than once – serially)
from the heart, trying to avoid cliche and maudlin stains
that cloy the finger-ridges till one print matches all.

later from the brain, a cold
cerebral summoning of impulses phalanxed
into lines, soldier jaws riveted to attention.

now I riddle intestinally, heart calcified
and mind axecuted wringing wry hands
like an errant queen. close examination

of digestive processes, awareness of ingest
and expel, wrinkling of nasal nous
until control is achieved, or at least,

approached. where it all comes from, goes?
a tentative trace shows words navigating
the bag of gut-whorls waltzing, worlding

kilter and skelter hither dither slither
emerging as *how the fuck?* and *what the fuck?*
hurled up against a barricade of stars.

Staccato for Lovers

No blades were sheathed, no target spared,
Throughout the cut and thrust we shared.
The bitter words like songbirds snared,
    And love was winged, as if lust cared.

For pleasure's course, you needed pain
To salt the cooling dish again.
I was too greedy to complain.
    When love is bleeding, lust may reign.

Like starving wolves we'd quickly rise,
And feast on flesh with hungry eyes,
With wanton tongues and carnal cries.
    Love ran the race; lust stole the prize.

No blades were sheathed, no target spared;
Dark wounds too deep to be repaired.
Our skin was flayed and bones were bared.
    Lust sucked the peach that love had pared.

The Stalker

He stands too close. I try to shift away.
He's like a seasoned groper on campaign.
I squirm. He salsas up a dark sashay
and always ends up close as sweat again.
I watch TV; his skull rolls in my lap
and sneers. I try to eat but choke and cough;
he clogs my throat. I lie in bed to nap;
he prods my lungs to check I don't nod off.

I'm mad. I want to send in a report
and have it stopped. I need the right address.
How can I get him banned? I'll phone the court.
Bring me Judge Dread and let me kneel, confess
to him that every bloody time I breathe
I hear the Reaper laughing up my sleeve.

Starlings

Words are translated into a tingle of wire,
faint jazz in the starlings' toes.
They perch on paragraphs, pleas,

punctuations, twanging on the taut lines.
Sometimes they splash-bomb the grass
or hack the air with harsh music.

They are the beat birds, vagabonds,
swaggerers, loud as peacock feathers.
ragged black and drab, swinging

between poles, rainbowed like oil on a wet road.
In the evening they rise and fly to secret roosts,
bearing messages. The wires are lighter

in the dark. Your voice sounds different
on the phone without the weight
of beaks and hollow bones.

Stepford Forded

When they had been married seven years
he locked her into the back bedroom
and came at night with a sterilised blade
to sever her head from her body.
After that she couldn't speak but still
she went out into the city each day
in a charcoal suit, the stump of her,
and her raw neck smiled at clients,
her blind hands ushered them along
corridors, her feet rowed on leather oars
past the congregation of frogs.

This is a swamp I can no longer smell,
she thought, turning the numb gold
circle on her finger. *This band squeezes
the main artery to my heart*, she thought,
*or would do if that had not collapsed
and bled into the fine Turkoman rug
by the bed that is as empty as my vessels.*
The stump healed. They made a prosthesis,
snug as a glove, which thought and spoke
and laughed for her. Its complexion was
flawless, its teeth were white and strong.
What more could a modern woman want?

A String of Pearls

'It is Margaret you mourn for'
                Gerald Manley Hopkins

I wish I had another name.
I wish I didn't feel the same
as all the others christened so.
In truth, I wish I didn't know
that all the Margarets, just as I,
will live and love and laugh and die.

Stroke

In his 45th year, my father was felled
by cerebral thrombosis, and lay on the tiled floor
like a storm-blasted oak. There was blood
where his temple had struck the stall-door.
They found him and carried him away
to be tubed and injected, shocked back
from another land. Once he told me stories
of a tribe of ants who lived under great roots.
He saw them again, waving their antennae
solemnly. I said, *I think a stroke first meant
you were stroked by God's hand*. I thought of Thor,
not Jehovah. My father never believed in God.

He was saved, with one side blurred.
Without the sinister side, he was no longer
my father. He sat in his wheelchair
like an emperor upon a dragon throne,
petulant as a bilious baby. I said, *if
you exercise, the muscles will work again*.
He did not believe me, any more than
he had believed the priests, or his dark-clad
aunts. His green hills never raised a saviour
amongst the drifts of sullen sheep.

Father, I am as empty of faith as you were,
but all my limbs function. I am full of the anger
in your genes. The ants are streaming through
my blood. They lift leaves, heavy as roofs.
They run. They survive. They are a black river
through the forest on the mountain
where you will never walk again.

Strutting the Strat

I love his brushwood chords,
his castaway voice, pushed back like
a roustabout's hat on his wild brown hair. He sings
plains blueing into distance, earth spirits,
the wheeling open road, and love
with a dark bandit sneer.

He sings the long low sky from state to state,
fierce colours in the desert, and beer-cans
rolling on the highway. An unwinged angel, he sings
learning to fly against the wind. Freedom strings
like silver between his widespread words.

Wasteland thrush, stray dog singer, rider
of lost ranges, he can push cities aside, swing
landscape open like a saloon door. When he whistles,
I hitch my hours to the rail, follow my nose
across mountains to the moment
where we spilled the gold-dust.

Studying Savonarola,
he considers his lover as kindling

With your amber eyes, yellow and red
of you, sun-sign heart like a blood orange
suspended in a porcelain cage, say you burn

in a courtyard and your ichor drips like honey
on the firewood, on the branches bound in fasces,
flesh fumed in the air, dark as molasses,

but what you are hovers as mist, as the spirit
of water is invisible until steam makes the sky
waver. Say you die, scorched into ashes, say

you pass from here to there, with your marigold
eyes, the garden darker for lack of one golden flower,
would bees mourn, would crickets keen, drawing long

blue chords on their thighs like cellists?
Say you disperse like petals on the wind,
the bright stem of you still a living stroke

in memory, still green, still spring, still the tint
and the tang of you in my throat, unconsumed.

A Sudden Sparrow

It lay against a garden wall, lids tight
as if the hidden eyes had never seen,
wings furled as though they'd never tasted flight,
beak sealed like new with amber lacquered sheen.
Long flawless feathers nestled glossy brown
unfanned, and on its sides, as finishing,
fresh chestnut dapples shone on dove-grey down;
each part seemed primed and poised to start and spring.

But dawn had sifted sun across its rest,
and it slept on. I knew its sight had chilled
on dark; the heart hung limp within its breast,
small lungs unsonged and slender claws unfilled –
yet still I waited for the bird to fly,
as if the trees concealed a greener sky.

Sunday Times

My door-mat's bare: no pages to enjoy.
I phone the shop. Last week they blamed the snow
but now a girl admits the Sunday boy
has let them down. Deliver-less, no show
for art reviews, for science updates, wars
and peace. No supplements, no insights now
on politics across the globe, no scores,
no crosswords to squinch tramlines in my brow.

I like to think his press-packed cycle veered
to church, and he has donned a seraph face
and dove-white robe, and is installed, choir-tiered,
to pipe *Pie Jesu* with fervent grace.

The world can wait, those tumbling words, that news.
I fill my room with Fauré's calm, and muse.

Sweeney in the Lady Chapel

Father, Son and Holy Ghost – praise God,
not one womb between them, unless
there is some uterine shape wavering in the Spirit,
but, adjusting our lenses, we think not.
This means not one spot of menstrual flux,
which is a good thing, monthly blood
being unclean, not shed by the hands or feet
or side, but by the leaking centre, the sink
and sump of corruption, the hole and haven
of original sin. Veil it, purge it, sew it up,
stamp on it for the width of mortal time.

Avoid the iron stench of it, the dark stain,
that moil and mutter of the nether mouth
which speaks to Satan, which is the gape
of hell, not the strait entrance to heaven.
Now let us pray, *Ave* to the Virgin Mary,
who was delivered of the Christ child
through the cockles of her right ear,
most becomingly and sweetly. *Ave*, Mother
undefiled, glory of folded flesh and fingers,
holy flower, everlasting maiden, who births
Powers from her salmon-pink tongue, who buds
Thrones and Seraphim between her pearly toes.

Switch

He jiggled his belt-purse and himportantly said,
Fix up your hair-hanks, your hexes, your traps,
mix up your unguents, your scallops and slaps.
Make me some magick to strike a crone dead.
I'm sick of my wife. I crave young flesh instead
so riffle your herbals, your Hecate-haps.
Go, whiffle your weirdings and Wiccaty-snaps
for there's a sweet morsel I'm bursting to bed.

I whistled the wainscot. Out popped a grey rat,
which was as thin as my client was fat.
I swapped their souls over, a straight tit for tat.
The new man sighed, *Thank you.* The rodent squeaked, *Bitch!*
One drawback to being a spotless white witch:
Though I charm like Calypso, I'll never get rich.

Take it from The End

I can tell you how I don't want this
to end. I don't want a red-tailed hawk
circling overhead, or the wind moving
through ash boughs, or anything
about the sea or sky. Spare me
the stars.

I can suggest how it could begin.
I'd sit here on this green chair,
with a coffee and a bar of chocolate,
thinking about a dream you had.
The dog would sleep on noisily,
as dogs do.

Outside in the garden, insects
would be scavenging the night.
If it rains, the soil will heave
with worms. I could step through
the door, and smell thyme breathing
by the path,

or I could sit on and drink
my coffee, pick up a book
and open it at a page
about heraldry or pigeons
or slavery in the Ottoman Empire –
because it will all be about
possibilities. It always is,
until the end.

Tantivvy

Hark, tantivvy on the breeze
stirs our ancient memories;
The baying of a pack of hounds,
one of earth's most glorious sounds.
I see pink men in full brave cry
and know the fox must love to die.
Let's raise the ruby stirrup cup
and toast to Reynard's ripping-up.
No more honorable employment
than to kill with sweet enjoyment.
Hark, tantivvy on the breeze:
Heaven is made of such as these.

Tarocchi

He made a tarot
in elaborate collage,
all the images cut out with a craftknife
from glossy pages –
articles, advertisements,
announcements –

precise as a surgeon
removing quick skin to be grafted.
None of the images were acknowledged
but they   niggled   at your sight.

Overhead a comet curled its tail
around the world once, twice,
growling and glowering
like a wounded dragon.

The sky bled and trumpets
ranged on the heights
blew war's clarion.
The emperor's horses
arched their throats.

All this was shown on the cards:
the crowds that shuffle through
the streets, flat as paper,
great cats that roam the hinterland
and feast on nomads,
jackals that fight over the remnants,
snarl to snout.

cut the deck
deal me a future
before I slip into my box
forever

Testimony

(Westminster Hall, January 1649)

Our monarch proved a traitor, so he came
to court, but still he did not recognise
the perils of his case. He thought his name
and rank must raise him safe, unscathed. All eyes
were fixed on him, and from his height of birth,
he looked on us, as I've eyed sheep and swine,
and no doubt judged our hides of little worth.
He yet believed his right to rule divine,

but such false pride provokes a sign from Thee.
The silver head drops from his cane. Its fall
rings out, but no man stoops for it. No knee
is bent. It rolls within plain sight of all.
Dear Lord, how such a petty, pretty thing
may teach a man he is no longer King!

Things I never asked for

I never asked for this, to be mortal,
to dream of Death and find him waiting for me
at the foot of the stairs, or sniffing the milk
in the fridge. I never asked for a list of losses,
to stand with bowed heart and see them
go down in ornamented timber like captain's chests.
I never asked for pain, for tears, for fears at night,
for the greyness in my head that bulges my eyes
into blurred words. I never asked for them, but I'm told
there are immortal ones asking for these things,
who never get them, who sit and cry for them,
like dogs scenting high bones, begging for them,
as a charm against the bliss and bland eternal.
Take them, you bastards, take them – I don't want
the weights in my knapsack, my suitcase of cares.

Thoughts from the hide.

He watches a blue-tit feeding
its young, the fledgling a blur
and gape and gulp of demand,
the adult bird infinitely flustered.
If a bird can frown, it frowns,
and seeps invisible sweat.
The tongue knows only four tastes,
salt, like re-routed tears,
acid, a dry suck of lemon,
bitter, the exudate of brilliant beetles,
and sweet like a strawberry shake
or his mother's milk
which he does not remember
but for which he feels suddenly grateful.

The blue-tit flies off to seek another bug,
another fat curl of caterpillar,
which will be as satisfying
as his mother's milk,
which he cannot remember.
The first flavour on his tongue
apart from its own familiar saliva,
was the taste of his mother's milk
which he cannot remember
but for which he is suddenly grateful.

The bird returns with a moth
as pale as milk, or moonlight.
The fledgling swallows it with a bulge
of eyeballs, then gapes again.

Throwaway lines

– for Sine the Brown

I'll lose some things I will not need:
that tag, these toys, this plaited lead.

I'll ditch some things I cannot use:
that dish, those cans, these rawhide chews.

I'll dump some things that make me weep:
those bones, this basket full of sleep –

and I'd bin this ache inside my chest
if I could bag it with the rest.

Tidings of Great Joy

God visited the poultry yard.
His knife was sharp. His eyes were hard.
He said, "While angels choir above,
sweet carollings of peace and love,
you will be plucked and roast and sliced."
The turkeys gulped, and groaned, "Oh, Christ!"

Times They Are A-Changin'

A big white van drives up, and slows. *Hi
there, love*, a young voice calls. I want to freeze
but trot. *Hey, talk to me.* I wave them by,
the little tykes, then see the badge. They're police.
Are you okay? Yes, fine. But they don't go.
A lone female...it's late... Some curfew now? God,
what cheek!, but I smile *Thanks* as if I don't know
they're bored, and have no criminals to prod.

I want to shout, *This is MY street, MY place;
move on, you pigs, and don't invade my space.
Do you think I'm on the bloody game?
Why not ring up Vice and check my name?
Tesco's open all night long. It's strange
I choose to shop at night? When did things change?*

Who decides now how I live my life?
Jeez, what if they'd frisked me, found my knife?

To a Lost Friend

I thought of you tonight and how
you'd taste this dish of mashed potatoes,
with the brown and green peppercorns
grated on its snow. It would remind you of winter days,
when we lavished white bread with butter,
and crammed hot mash between the slices.
Anchor dribbled down our chins like guilt and honey.
We laughed and made strong bowls of Assam tea
to wash it down, licked our fingers, and revelled
in warmth. We were cats then with electric fur.

Later we became human and tangled apart.
Still, I write for you, recall your basic pleasures,
wish you were here to sugar my tea. As we grow,
we gain and we lose, we turn final pages
and the periods tear our vision like tiny bullets.
I long for the story that never ends,
the teller who squats in the sun like a basking lizard.
The simple joy of his tongue, the subtle pattern
of his scales. I want you to sit beside me, listening
to the tale. After a while I will take your hand and step inside.

To His Boy Mistress

Had we but World enough, and Time,
your dress-sense, Laddie, were no crime.
But since Time's tongue is always curt,
I wish you'd drop that micro-skirt.

Tom's Credo

A dog with an egg in its mouth. Mountains built on a city.
Seven books bound in calfskin. Lightning sheets like intermittent dawn.

A wet heart between wings of bone. Kittens suckling a quean.
An eternity ring set with stories. Music through closed doors.

A seraph's fingers plucking strings. Blood on marble. Rain.
An ecstasy of roses. Recognising a stranger. Twelve precepts.

Creamed potatoes on a porcelain dish. Silver knives. Riddles.
Russian dolls. The scent of violets. White horses in the surf.

A tapestry hung with pomegranates. Musk apples. Milk in a bucket.
Mozart. Raphael. A great rock at the end of the world.

To those in the air.

I am on the ground.
one of the underpeople
who hears an explosion
and feels the blast.

From above it is a puff of smoke,
a pepper of dust.
Fly away, and leave us
to comfort the girl who screams
because she cannot find
her legs and the man
who bubbles sound
without teeth or a tongue.

High in the air
there is no smell,
just the sweet rush of air,
the neat phrases
on the radio.
It must be like having wings.

To Tim

Some authors don't rebel,
and meekly meet the night.
There's more ink in your well
so write, you bastard, write.

Traditions

One day when my grandmother was visiting, she stroked my hair and my face, and said to my mother, "Child, your daughter is becoming a woman." I was pleased but my mother frowned. She did not smile. It puzzled me.

That evening my mother and father had a big argument. I heard their loud voices long after I went to bed. In the morning they went on, shouting in whispers so I could not hear. My father said, "No, I will not agree to it. That is my decision". My mother folded her arms and her lips, and said nothing more.

Two months later, it was the start of the long holiday. No school for weeks ahead. I was happy, and danced home, swinging my bag. When I arrived, Grandma was there, and my aunt Safira. My mother looked worried. Grandma took me by the hand and said she had a surprise for me.

Outside was a big dusty black car, and waiting inside were Nurse Hani, the midwife, and some other women. They drove me to a place I did not know. They stripped me and held me down and Nurse did it with a razor blade. I screamed and screamed with pain till the screaming nearly made me sick, but they did not stop.

I cried out, "Why are you hurting me? Why are you doing this to me?" Aunt Safira said, "Hush, it is for your good." Grandma said "You want to be married, don't you, Amele? You don't want to disgrace our family?"

Afterwards Nurse sewed me up and bound my legs together to try and stop the bleeding. They drove me home. My mother was weeping. I hated her. I hated my Grandma and my aunt and Nurse Hani. I hated everybody. I lay in my bed, bleeding and hating.

When my father got home, I heard him shouting very loudly. After that, there was silence. Then my father came to me, sat on my bed and held my hand. I cried hard, with hot tears, and he rocked me, and called me his Amele, his baby.

328

Tried and true

I want to be tried in the U.S. of A.
I want to be tried on tv.
I want a defender in seams and high heels
so the people aren't looking at me.

I want a jury made up of all men,
twelve citizens trusted and true.
I want an attorney in micro and silk
so the jurors will know what to do.

I want to be tried in the U.S. of A.
I want to be tried on tv.
I want my sweet lawyer to point out the fact
that Society's guilty – not me.

I want to be clean-shaved, dark-suited and smart,
and then if they send me to pen,
I'll campaign for justice from behind bars
and soon have my freedom again.

I want to be tried in the U.S. of A.
I want to be tried on tv.
America knows we're all victims not perps,
so that's where a good boy should be.

The Turquoise Bear

Chained around my neck I wear
the totem of a rearing bear;
I walk on two legs like a man
but I have quit the human clan.
You may think you know me well
but I despise your soapy smell.

As I stroll through city streets
my blood is dark with hot fierce beats.
While I talk in cultured tones,
my teeth are white from gnawing bones.
When I pay with crisp green notes,
my mind is red with severed throats.

untitled ... 1

Fucking fuck haiku,
fucking fuck senryu
and fucking fuck you too!

untitled ... 2

Hedgehog-hair, and just one sandal,
My muse is scarcely worth the candle.
She is a lax and sullen bitch,
But useful when I get the itch.

untitled ... 3

The Invisible Man came to rue
The day he gave Catgirl a screw.
He got crushed by the bulk
Of the Incredible Hulk
Who'd decided to roger her too.

A Valentina

When I'm with you, I hum.
I'm a bee drunk on buddleia,
I buzz. I'm a thrush full of snails,
I sing. Like a creamery cat,
I purr. I'm a mucky pup,
I roll. I'm wildlife, I'm tame,
I'm a verb, reverberating.

A Victim's Voice

I was killed by hate
that festered through long years.
Wrap me in your love,
wash me with your tears.

I was killed by hate
but love had shaped my life:
sibling, colleague, friend,
parent, child, and wife

I was killed by hate
but do not let hate win;
think of the human heart
that beats beneath the skin.

I was killed by hate
that burnt away my breath.
Remember me in life;
don't bury me with death.

A View from the Hill

(Where do we go when the world forsakes us?
Where the healing waters flow. – Mister Mister)

Consider the fortunate: those golden souls
who never lose the sun, or never for more than
a short season. Their rain is always summer-soft,
their skies always blink blue. Their eggs hatch.
What of the rest of us, disconnected, feeling
the cold spaces of the stars so keenly,
we rarely look up? We know there is a festival

somewhere where music is loud and wine fountains,
where their gods look down with embracing smiles,
where the favoured are flushed with warmth.
We never receive an invitation. Sometimes we hear
faint strains streets away, sometimes we catch a glitter
in our eyes' corners, but the feast is elusive. We put
our feelers down, we forage for crumbs. We work.
We are iron and tin and bronze, cheap alloy,

but life grants us instants of joy, pangs and flutterings
in the ribs as if the heart can fly out of its cage.
More and more I am seized by these mundane ecstacies,
sweet yet bewildering. I have no god, no guardians,
or none that I know. Who is the stranger who visits me?
Whose is the voice I understand but do not hear?
In my tall twisted colony, I start to dream of a spring
at the earth's core, the enigmatic bliss.

Vigil

On the pale shaft of beach, I wait,
the harsh high chalk behind me.
The boy fidgets, racks his throat,
reams nostrils for hidden gold, gropes
his crotch for Christ knows what.
The pony snorts, snickers, shakes its head
The boy told me it had been down a pit
pulling tin-ore. I imagine them dark
and hunched like dwarves, drawing it
brownbellied like a swollen bucket
up from a well. The fever in my arm
is heating my brain. God's guts,
I hate this sullen sodden race
spawned by a land below a leaden sky.
I dream of fragrant citrus leaves,
the aromatic ball of bay that crowns
a topiary garden, loud parrots
fed fruit ripe from tropick isles,
Moorish girls quiet as voles, dark
and sweet as caramel, the swirl
of bright fabric, white teeth in brown skin,
sun, by God, the blessed sun
which some men worship as a deity.
Heretics, but this misbelief no more sinful
than these white devils with their bleary light.
The pain from wrist to shoulder,
soon I will be home and warm, drinking
ruby wine, hearing fierce melodies
celebrating our victory. Philip will smash
their ships, burn their ports, humble their
mannish queen in honour of the Faith.

The pony snuffs the air. I hear
myself telling the boy, "Make sure
you keep the beast above ground.
Do not send it down into the dark again."
I give him coins. Feel the gold
as cool in my palm as the fire
in my forearm is hot. Soon, I know
it will be soon. Salve, Regina,
mater misericordiae.

Visiting the Surgical Ward

I come festooned with flowers, smiles and grapes,
prepared to play my part, to entertain
and act the fool, a cheery jackanapes
with jokes and japes. I know I must sustain
a jester's role and this façade can't fail
despite the rictus of a monkey grin.
Give me a short red coat that bares my tail
and I will caper like a capuchin

but better that than show the dog behind
my eyes, that blackly hunkers down and whines.
It would attack if only it could find
an enemy to bite. Instead it pines;
for neither simian nor hound can tell
if this goodbye will be our last farewell.

Vix

Vix the victim
Vix the persecuted
Vix the ancient presence
torn, tormented, taunted
labelled vile and verminous
by a destroying race
hunted, disinterred,
killed by close kin, cubs
clubbed for sport
I hail

Vix the vigilant
Vix the predator
Vix the shadow made flesh
in town in country on the city streets
who watches me approaching
snuffs with berrybright nose
with the sage, sharp mask
scans and reads me
as no threat
I hail

Vix the prowler
Vix the valiant
Vix the cunning heart
who comes from earth
deep in treeroots and ferns
glides russet across the ground
on dainty feet, half dog, half deer
with the old wisdom
in his gaze
I hail

Vix enduring
Vix victorious
Vix the arrow of the land
ebony tipped and nailed
autumn apple forest spirit
call to your brethren
from shire to shire
red beast of Albion, wait
until the king returns
to greet you
in your rich dark realm

Walking Canford Heath

I am writing this with gritted teeth
and hope I don't sound bitter,
but I'd like to see more blasted heath
and far less blasted litter.

The Wall Behind the Paintings

I am tired of people talking about heart and art,
yabbing of their insights and sensibilities,
that they are more More than the common flock,
the herd of greylings in the grind, grounded

in the ordinary. Catch these beauties, who have
Soul. It lingers in the interstices of long
sentences, broken, not with sighs, but with
the shadow of soughs. A sigh would not be subtle

enough. A certain fat silence is good.
They have significances dripping like gems
from their gestures, like fat baroque pearls
that iridesce resentfully, as if they are too

exquisite to conform to a mere sphere.
I am sick of special people, with their paints
and blades, their pharmacopeia of words
to salve and solve the world. I no longer

have faith in their knowledge or visions.
They shit and piss like the rest of you,
and die with the same *What the fuck
is this?* in their oh-so-precious eyes.

Water Wings

In the river, I float paper boats. They skim over the pebbles
in the shallows like white butterflies. Tu Fu asks me
where I find the paper. I tell him the boats are poems.

Ah, he replies. No, I say, the poems are printed
on the paper. See, the letters swim like ants
through young rice. Tu Fu purses his lips. and pushes

back his reed-weaved hat. These poems? he begins.
My friend, I say, sit and share with me the fragrance of dark tea.
I pour the liquid into a fine chrysanthemum bowl.

He sips like a carp nibbling pondweed. These poems?
he repeats. Do not worry, I say. People write so many.
More arrive every day, flights of crane in my mail.

They are all 'After Li Po'. They all speak of this village.
I weary of them, so I send them down the singing stream.
Indeed, Tu Fu says, white butterflies are better.

The Weather Man

In the last wood, he waits.
The leaves of his hair
are crisp with frost.
Old air is bleak along
the withered limbs.

He cranes his senses
for the echo
of sundered voices,
but only the wind speaks
and it has no language.

This is a ward, they said,
but he can see the trunks
decaying, smell
the rotting roots.
He has come to this,
the final winter

and weather is blowing
all the words away
into swirls of snow.
They cannot touch him
in his coldness
or breach the white wall.

So, he thinks,
as it ends,
shedding a tear
of ragged ice
for the world,
the world lost,
and all the warmth
wasted.

Wisdom from the Butt

Do not talk about words,
write.

Do not discuss your intentions,
act.

Do not worry about God,
live.

Do not frown about tomorrow,
dance.

Witch

Small Mercy Mary Erkinshaw, who saw
the gleam of bones in birches, and who heard
the honey in the raven's bitter caw,
grew lithe as cat, and sweetmouthed as a bird.
The midwife sealed the caul that marked her strange,
with muttered words, inside a stoneware jar.
Bright-haired, fey-eyed, light-limbed, she loved to range
the deepness of the woods and greet each star.

She knew the places where earth's secrets lurk;
each twilight she heard owlets scritch her name
and tip tip tip of Waylan's hammerwork
as he forged metal tears in future flame.
Still Mercy healed snapped wings, kissed mice and toads,
and followed hooves and horns down midnight roads.

Wolves

Wolves each end
and the world
is piggy-in-the-middle.

The Women's Circle

Faith takes the chair, and switches off her phone,
"First, gifts for our poor sisters overseas:
Joy has donated three warm wraps, and Joan,
a book entitled *Women: Off Your Knees!*"
Amanda checks her hair, Sue clears her plate
and Caitlin thrums her throat to signal hush:
'Anent last month's pornography debate
I'll show a tape to illustrate this trash.'

Faith views the tilting pricks and shaven groins,
tuts with the others at the sordid scene,
the squalid pumping of the actors' loins.
Stern-faced she watches like a widowed queen
and feels with pique, as personal affront,
the creeping liquefaction of her cunt.

Writer's Block

I cannot pen a poem:
my Muse is up the spout.
I cannot pen a poem;
the words will not come out.

I cannot pen a poem;
my brain is in a tizz.
I cannot pen a poem
but, fuck me, here it is.

Wunderkind

Girls shouldn't follow rabbits
down the tunnel of their fears.
Nurse warned that such bad habits
will always end in tears.

One child found her world absurd
and faced a stacked royal deck.
Games of man and beast and bird
kept words and dreams in check.

She stood neat-socked, in blue,
as innocent as Bambi:
if wisdom takes a wide-eyed view,
nimbly namby-pamby?

I sometimes think of Alice
seeking logic, home and truth,
oblivious of the malice
that chokes the hopes of youth.

Stout Tweedledum and Tweedledee
explained things tit for tat.
My faith has faded in a tree;
it grimaced like a cat.

As the stone Mad Hatter laughs,
the Walrus weeps salt pearls;
the White Knight paws old photographs
fleshed out with little girls.

Yam Sandwich

I am, I am, I am...what?
Better to tell you what I'm not.

Wiser to fish inside my mind
and air whatever crumbs I find.
Crumbs will serve to feed the birds
which flick their tails at fancy words.
Sparrows, songlarks, thrushes, wrens,
nestlings, fledglings, cocks and hens –

They are, they are, they are...what?
Full of secrets I forgot.